Recovery of Faith

BY S. RADHAKRISHNAN

An Idealist View of Life
The Hindu View of Life
The Bhagavadgita
Religion and Society
The Concept of Man
The Principal Upanisads

Recovery

of

Faith

RADHAKRISHNAN

INDUS

An imprint of HarperCollins *Publishers* India

INDUS
An imprint of HarperCollins *Publishers* India Pvt Ltd
7/16 Ansari Road, New Delhi 110 002

Published by Indus 1994

First published in Great Britain 1956

ISBN 81-7223-145-8

Printed in India by
Gopsons Papers Pvt Ltd
A-28 Sector IX
Noida 201 301

CONTENTS

World Perspectives

WORLD PERSPECTIVES is dedicated to the concept of man born out of a universe perceived through a fresh vision of reality. Its aim is to present short books written by the most conscious and responsible minds of today. Each volume represents the thought and belief of each author and sets forth the interrelation of the changing religious, scientific, artistic, political, economic and social influences upon man's total experience.

This Series is committed to a re-examination of all those sides of human endeavor which the specialist was taught to believe he could safely leave aside. It interprets present and past events impinging on human life in our growing World Age and envisages what man may yet attain when summoned by an unbending inner necessity to the quest of what is most exalted in him. Its purpose is to offer new vistas in terms of world and human development while refusing to betray the intimate correlation between universality and individuality, dynamics and form, freedom and destiny. Each author treats his subject from the broad perspective of the world community, not from the Judaeo-Christian, Western, or Eastern viewpoint alone.

Certain fundamental questions which have received too little consideration in the face of the spiritual, moral and political world crises of our day, and in the light of technology which has released the creative energies of peoples, are treated in these books. Our authors deal with the increasing realization that spirit and nature are not separate and apart; that intuition and reason must regain their importance as the means of perceiving and fusing inner being with outer reality.

World Perspectives endeavors to show that the conception of organism is a higher and more concrete conception than that of matter and energy. Thus it would seem that science itself must ultimately pursue the aim of interpreting the physical world of matter and energy in terms of the biological conception of organism. An enlarged meaning of life, of biology, not as it is revealed in the test tube of the laboratory but as it is experienced within the organism of life itself is presented in this Series. For the principle of life consists in the tension which connects spirit with the realm of matter. The element of life is dominant in the very texture of nature, thus rendering life, biology, a trans-empirical science. The laws of life have their origin beyond their mere physical manifestations and compel us to consider their spiritual source. In fact, the widening of the conceptual framework has not only served to restore order within the respective branches of knowledge, but has also disclosed analogies in man's position regarding the analysis and synthesis of experience in apparently separated domains of knowledge suggesting the possibility of an ever more embracing objective description.

Knowledge, it is shown, no longer consists in a manipulation of man and nature as opposite forces, nor in the reduction of data to mere statistical order, but is a means of liberating mankind from the destructive power of fear, pointing the way toward the goal of the rehabilitation of the human will and the rebirth of faith and confidence in the human person. The works published also endeavor to reveal that the cry for patterns, systems and authorities is growing less insistent as the desire grows stronger in both East and West for the recovery of a dignity, integrity and self-realization which are the inalienable rights of man who may now guide change by means of conscious purpose in the light of rational experience.

Other vital questions explored relate to problems of international understanding as well as to problems dealing with prejudice and the resultant tensions and antagonisms. The growing perception and responsibility of our World Age point to the new reality that the individual person and the collective person supplement and integrate each other; that the thrall of totalitarianism of both right and left has been shaken in the universal desire to recapture the authority of truth and human totality. Mankind can finally place its trust not in a proletarian authoritarianism, not in a secularized humanism, both of which have betrayed the spiritual property right of history, but in a sacramental brotherhood and in the unity of knowledge, a widening of human horizons beyond every parochialism, and a revolution in human thought comparable to the basic assumption, among the ancient Greeks, of the sovereignty of reason; corresponding to the great effulgence of the moral conscience articulated by the Hebrew prophets; analogous to the fundamental assertions of Christianity; or to the beginning of a new scientific era, the era of the science of dynamics, the experimental foundations of which were laid by Galileo in the Renaissance.

An important effort of this Series is to re-examine the contradictory meanings and applications which are given today to such terms as democracy, freedom, justice, love, peace, brotherhood and God. The purpose of such inquiries is to clear the way for the foundation of a genuine *world* history not in terms of nation or race or culture but in terms of man in relation to God, to himself, his fellow man and the universe, that reach beyond immediate self-interest. For the meaning of the World Age consists in respecting man's hopes and dreams which lead to a deeper understanding of the basic values of all peoples.

Today in the East and in the West men are discovering that they are bound together, beyond any divisiveness, by a more fundamental unity than any mere agreement in thought and doctrine. They are beginning to know that all men possess the same primordial desires and tendencies; that the domination of man over man can no longer be justified by any appeal to God or nature; and such consciousness is the fruit of the spiritual and moral revolution through which humanity is now passing.

World Perspectives is planned to gain insight into the meaning of man, who not only is determined by history but who also determines history. History is to be understood as concerned not only with the life of man on this planet but as including also such cosmic influences as interpenetrate our human world.

This generation is discovering that history does not conform to the social optimism of modern civilization and that the organization of human communities and the establishment of justice, freedom and peace are not only intellectual achievements but spiritual and moral achievements as well, demanding a cherishing of the wholeness of human personality and constituting a never-ending challenge to man, emerging from the abyss of meaninglessness and suffering, to be renewed and replenished in the totality of his life. "For as one's thinking is, such one becomes, and it is because of this that thinking should be purified and transformed, for were it centered upon truth as it is now upon things perceptible to the senses, who would not be liberated from his bondage." [1]

There is in mankind today a counterforce to the sterility and danger of a quantitive, anonymous mass culture, a new, if sometimes imperceptible, spiritual sense of convergence toward world unity on the basis of the sacredness of each human person and respect for the plurality of cultures. There is a growing awareness that equality and justice are not to be evaluated in mere numerical terms but that they are proportionate and analogical in their reality.

We stand at the brink of the age of the world in which human life presses forward to actualize new forms. The false separation of man and nature, of time and space, of freedom and security, is acknowledged and we are faced with a new vision of man in his organic unity and of history offering a richness and diversity of quality and majesty of scope hitherto unprecedented. In relating the accumulated wisdom of man's spirit to the new reality of the World Age, in articulating its thought and belief, *World Perspectives* seeks to encourage a renaissance of hope in society and of pride in man's decision as to what his destiny will be.

The experience of dread, in the pit of which contemporary man has been plunged through his failure to transcend his existential limits, is the experience of the problem of whether he shall attain to being through the knowledge of himself or shall not, whether he shall annihilate nothingness or whether nothingness shall annihilate him. For he has been forced back to his origins as a result of the atrophy of meaning, and his anabasis may begin once more through his mysterious greatness to re-create his life.

[1] Maitri Upanishad, 6, 34, 4, 6.

The suffering and hope of this century have their origin in the interior drama in which the spirit is driven as a result of the split within itself, and in the invisible forces which are born in the heart and mind of man. This suffering and this hope arise also from material problems, economic, political, technological. History itself is not a mere mechanical unfolding of events in the center of which man finds himself as a stranger in a foreign land. The specific modern emphasis on history as progressive, the specific prophetic emphasis on God as acting through history, and the specific Christian emphasis on the historical nature of revelation must now surrender to the new history embracing the new cosmology—a profound event which is in the process of birth in the womb of that invisible universe which is the mind of man.

This is the crisis in consciousness made articulate through the crisis in science. This is the new awakening after a long history which had its genesis in Descartes' denial that theology could exist as a science, on the one hand, and on the other, in Kant's denial that metaphysics could exist as a science. Some fossilized forms of such positivistic thinking still remain. However, it is now conceded, out of the influences of Whitehead, Bergson, and some phenomenologists, that in addition to natural science with its tendency to isolate quantitative values there exists another category of knowledge wherein philosophy, utilizing its own instruments, is able to grasp the essence and innermost nature of the Absolute, of reality. The mysterious universe is now revealing to philosophy and to science as well an enlarged meaning of nature and of man which extends beyond mathematical and experimental analysis of sensory phenomena. This meaning rejects the mechanistic conception of the world and that positivistic attitude toward the world which considers philosophy as a kind of mythology adequate only for the satisfaction of emotional needs. In other words, the fundamental problems of philosophy, those problems which are central to life, are again confronting science and philosophy itself. Our problem is to discover a principle of differentiation and yet relationship lucid enough to justify and to purify both scientific and philosophical knowledge by accepting their mutual interdependence.

Justice itself, which has been "in a state of pilgrimage and crucifixion" and now is slowly being liberated from the grip of social and political demonologies in the East as well as in the West, begins to question its own premises. Those modern revolutionary movements which have challenged the sacred institutions of society by protecting social injustice in the name of social justice are also being examined and re-evaluated.

When we turn our gaze retrospectively to the early cosmic condition of man in the third millennium, we observe that the concept of justice as something to which man has an inalienable right began slowly to take form and, at the time of Hammurabi in the second millennium, justice, as inherently a part of man's nature and not as a beneficent gift to be bestowed, became part of the consciousness of society. This concept of human rights consisted in the demand for justice in the universe, a demand which exists again in the twentieth century through a curious analogy. In accordance with the ancient view, man could himself become a god, could assume the identity of the great cosmic forces in the universe which surrounded him. He could influence this universe, not by supplication, but by action. And now again this consciousness of man's just relationship with the universe, with society and with his fellow men, can be actualized, and again not through supplication but through action.

Though never so powerful materially and technologically, Western democracy, with its concern for the sacredness of the human person gone astray, has never before been so seriously threatened morally and spiritually. National security and individual freedom are in ominous conflict. The possibility of a universal community and the technique of degradation exist side by side. There is no doubt that evil is accumulated among men in their passionate desire for unity. And yet, confronted with this evil, confronted with death, man, from the very depths of his soul, cries out for justice. Christianity in history could only reply to this protest against evil by the Annunciation of the Kingdom, by the promise of Eternal Life—which demanded faith. But the spiritual and moral suffering of man exhausted his faith and his hope. He was left alone. His suffering remained unexplained.

However, man has now reached the last extremity of denigration. He yearns to consecrate himself. And so, among the spiritual and moral ruins of the West and of the East a renaissance is prepared beyond the limits of nihilism, darkness and despair. In the depths of the spiritual night, civilization with its many faces turning toward its source, may rekindle its light in an imminent second dawn—even as in the last book of Revelation, which speaks of a Second Coming with a New Heaven, a New Earth, and a new religious quality of life.

> And I saw a new heaven and a new
> earth; for the first heaven and the
> first earth were passed away.[2]

[2] Revelation 21:1.

In spite of the infinite obligation of men and in spite of their finite power, in spite of the intransigence of nationalisms, and in spite of spiritual bereavement and moral decay, beneath the apparent turmoil and upheaval of the present, and out of the transformations of this dynamic period with the unfolding of a world consciousness, the purpose of *World Perspectives* is to help quicken the "unshaken heart of well-rounded truth" and interpret the significant elements of the World Age now taking shape out of the core of that undimmed continuity of the creative process which restores man to mankind while deepening and enhancing his communion with the universe.

New York, 1955

RUTH NANDA ANSHEN

Introduction

SENSITIVE and informed minds believe that the fundamental need of the world, far deeper than any social, political
or economic readjustment, is a spiritual reawakening, a recovery of faith. Great movements of spirit arise when despair
at the breakdown of civilisation makes the mind susceptible to
the recognition of the insufficiency of the existing order and
the need for rethinking its foundations and shifting its bases.
Science with its new prospect of a possible liquidation of the
world by man's own wanton interference reminds us of the
warning that the wages of sin is death.

The feeling that we have reached a decisive moment in our
history, that we have to make a choice that will determine the
course of events for centuries, is not peculiar to our times.
Many other epochs in history have held such a belief correctly
or incorrectly and each epoch has felt that it had more justification than most for making this claim. When Rome fell
Augustine cried: "The whole world groaned at the fall of
Rome." "The human race is included in the ruin; my tongue
cleaves to the roof of my mouth and sobs choke my words to
think that the city is a captive which led captive the whole
world," wrote St. Jerome from his monastery at Bethlehem.
About a millennium earlier, Thucydides spoke in sad terms of

1

the downfall of the Athenian Empire in the Peloponnesian
War of 431 to 404 B.C. An ancient Egyptian papyrus dating
from more than four thousand years ago contains the following passages:

> Robbers abound. . . . No one ploughs the land. People
> are saying: 'We do not know what will happen from day
> to day.' . . . Dirt prevails everywhere, and no longer does
> any one wear clean raiment. . . . The country is spinning
> round and round like a potter's wheel. . . . Slave-women
> are wearing necklaces of gold and lapis lazuli. No more do
> we hear any one laugh. . . . Great men and small agree in
> saying: 'Would that I had never been born.' . . . Well-
> to-do persons are set to turn millstones. . . . Ladies have to
> demean themselves to the tasks of serving-women. . . .
> People are so famished that they snatch what falls from the
> mouths of swine. . . . The offices where records are kept
> have been broken into and plundered . . . and the docu-
> ments of the scribes have been destroyed. . . . Moreover,
> certain foolish persons have bereft the country of the mon-
> archy; . . . the officials have been driven hither and thither;
> . . . no public office stands open where it should, and the
> masses are like timid sheep without a shepherd. . . . Artists
> have ceased to ply their art. . . . The few slay the many.
> . . . One who yesterday was indigent is now wealthy, and
> the sometime rich overwhelm him with adulation. . . . Im-
> pudence is rife. . . . Oh that man could cease to be, that
> women should no longer conceive and give birth. Then, at
> length, the world would find peace.[1]

Man's memory makes him aware of the age of his race so that
now as two thousand years ago or four thousand years ago he

[1] Selections from Erman's *Die Literatur der Aegypten* (1923), pp.
130–48. Quoted in Karl Jaspers, *Man in the Modern Age* (1951), p. 24,
Introduction.

feels that he is living in a terminal period. But formerly when civilisations were destroyed in one or more continents, in other regions they survived and the accumulated knowledge of the past enabled our brethren to save the future of the race. The Egyptian, the Greek and the Graeco-Roman civilisations belonged to small parts of the world, areas which did not comprise the whole of mankind. The forces of modern civilisation are world-wide. Again, when other civilisations collapsed the attack came mainly from without; today the menace is from within. The world is undergoing changes so vast that they are hardly comparable to the changes which occurred in the past. The contemporary situation is pregnant with great possibilities, immense dangers or immeasurable rewards. It may be the end or a new beginning. The human race may end by destroying itself or its spiritual vitality may revive and a new age may dawn when this earth will become a real home for humanity. The contemporary mind is vacillating between vague apocalyptic fears and deep mystical yearnings.

A world in arms divided into two apparently irreconcilable camps, each preparing to fling itself on the other, dominates our thoughts and emotions. The shape of the future gives us much concern. With all the resources at our command, with all the gifts with which we have been endowed, with all the powers that we have developed, we are unable to live in peace and safety. We have grown in knowledge and intelligence but not in wisdom and virtue. For lack of the latter, things are interlocked in perpetual strife. No centre holds the world together. Religion has been the discipline hitherto used for fostering wisdom and virtue. But the drift from religious belief has gone much too far and the margin of safety has become dangerously small. The social pathos of the age is exploited by countless individuals in different parts of the world who pose as leaders and proclaim their foolishness as wisdom. We are sowing grain and weeds at random.

It is no comfort to think that the sense of insecurity, of impending doom, of the scourge of war have afflicted successive generations of men ever since Cain slew Abel. So it has been from the beginning of time; but need it be so to the end of the world? [2] To believe that it is a law of nature, an edict of Providence by whose decree we are forever bound is to contradict man's inmost being. If life, as A. N. Whitehead says, is an offensive against the repetitive mechanism of the universe, human life is much more so. Man is not at the mercy of inexorable fate. If he *wills*, he can improve on his past record. There is no inevitability of history. To assume that we are helpless creatures caught in the current which is sweeping us into the final abyss is to embrace a philosophy of despair, of nihilism. We can swim against the current and even change its direction.

A false concept of history is corrupting the minds of men. It makes little difference whether the corruption is effected in the name of divine predestination or a law of inevitable progress to perfection, or a *Weltgeist*, or a classless society dialectically driving history towards its final consummation or by destiny presiding over a cycle of dramas which are all variations on a common theme. For Calvin the ultimate reality is the divine will, inscrutable and unapproachable.[3] God is all;

[2] Cf. Major-General J. F. C. Fuller: "There has never been a period in human history altogether free from war, and seldom one of more than a generation which has not witnessed a major conflict: great wars flow and ebb almost as regularly as the tides." *The Decisive Battles of the Western World* (1954), Vol. I, p. xi.

[3] "When we attribute fore-knowledge to God," wrote Calvin, "we mean that all things are always and perpetually under his eyes, though, to his

man is nothing. If he had not willed to save some, they never could have emerged from their doom. He elects some to life and judges others to death. If humanity lies in ruins, it is because of divine judgment. Like all fatalistic creeds Calvinism bids the soul endure its own helplessness. For Kant, history is the gradual moralisation of man, the working out of a divine purpose. History, for Hegel, is the progressive unfold-ment of the Absolute. By and large, mankind has moved to-wards equality and de Tocqueville felt that progress towards equality had all the characteristics of a divine decree: "It is universal, it is durable, it eludes all human interference." [4] The biological theory of evolution and the triumphs of science led to a buoyant belief in progress, though no law or automatic progress could be scientifically established. Spencer held that everything including humanity got automatically better and better. Marxists look forward to an age when "the true realm of freedom will blossom out of the realm of necessity in the fully developed communist society of the future." [5] Though Marx insists on the dialectical march of historical forces, he does not overlook the need for individual effort. Communists work in the belief that history is on their side. Nietzsche be-came convinced that the culture of Europe was doomed, that an eclipse of all traditional values was at hand and that we had strayed into a wilderness without path or guidance. Destiny has decreed, says Spengler, that our spiritual values should be frustrated in this period of history. We have to join the enemies of freedom, lend the Absolute Dialectic or history a hand in its

knowledge, there is no future or past, but only present. And this extends to the whole ambit of the universe and to all creatures."

[4] Preface to Part I, *Democracy in America*, trans. by Henry Reeve (1835).

[5] See Morris Ginsberg, *The Idea of Progress* (1953), p. 13.

business. We seem to have become apathetic, even cynical, and certain that no action of ours can prevent the triumph of evil we see around us.

Determinist views of history do not have an adequate idea of human freedom. Their vision is lacking in depth and dignity. They have no perception of the struggle of man under the shadow of necessity. Without faith in the free spirit of man we will become to ourselves what nature and history have become to us, a wilderness, a chaos. Karma can be overcome by freedom. Historical necessity can be overcome by a free act of spirit. "God has decided to destroy the Temple. In the name of God, rescue the temple from the wrath of God." Man has to travel the path which leads him from the basest in his nature upward to the noblest that raises him above his animality. The human individual is not a mere object among objects, a thing among things, without meaning for himself. He is not a psychological process which is completely conditioned. He is a victim of karma or necessity, if he is objectified and deprived of his subjectivity. It is possible for man to escape from the objective happenings. He can be himself. The whole history of mankind is a continuous endeavour to be free. The great lights in human form, the Buddha, Socrates, Zoroaster, Jesus, reveal to us the divine possibilities of human nature and give us the courage to be ourselves.

Progress in the past has not been continuous. Advance in one direction has sometimes meant deterioration in another. In moulding the material environment, we have made great advances, but in improving human relations, we have not. There does not seem to be any fixed law, plan or pattern in the course of history. Humanity moves forward by a series of jumps caused by man's free action. When we are conscious of

the present situation, it means that we can act in it purpose-
fully. The situation does not lead on to anything fixed and
fated. The trend to annihilation is not inevitable. The future
depends on what we think and will. To grasp the nature of the
situation is the first step towards mastering it. To understand
it rouses the will to modify it. We can make the pace as slow
or as swift as we like. There is so much inconsequence in our
lives that we cannot forecast the future with certainty.

Change is the law of life. Man has to adapt himself to the
conditions about him. When he is surrounded by water, he
becomes a fisherman living on what the sea supplies. If he lives
in a tropical climate with its luxuriant growth, he becomes a
fruit gatherer. Man has to come to terms with outside nature
and with himself. That is the condition of his survival. All religions proclaim as their goal the unification of humanity. This
has taken place in the physical or geographical sense but our
minds and hearts are yet to be prepared for the acceptance of
this oneness of humanity. A new orientation is required to
build a unity out of the divisions of races and peoples, out of
the rivalries of nations and conflicts of religions. This requires
a courageous effort and a radical change in our outlook.

Man cannot live and work without the hope that humanity
is really capable of rising to a higher moral plane; without the
dream that, in the end, he and his fellow mortals will be reconciled and will understand one another. There exist bonds as
well as barriers between individuals and nations. But mankind's highest destiny is to become more humane, more spiritual, more capable of sympathetic understanding. This hope
rises strong in the human heart, in periods like the present,
when confusion and horror are abroad.

The great religious teachers of the world preach something

different from the traditions they inherit. The seers of the Upaniṣads, Gautama the Buddha, Zoroaster, Socrates, Jesus, Muhammad, Nānak and Kabīr had to undergo in their lives an inevitable breakaway from the traditional views. Even as the seers of the Upaniṣads and the Buddha protested against Vedic ceremonialism, even as Jesus denounced Rabbinical orthodoxy, we have to protect the enduring substance of religion from the forms and institutions which suffer from the weaknesses of man and the corruptions of time. We must get away from a religion which has lost the power of creative expression in conformity with the needs and demands of our age. Kālidāsa in his *Mālavikāgnimitra* says: "Everything is not good simply because it is old; no literature should be treated as unworthy simply because it is new. Great men accept the one or the other after due examination. [Only] the fool has his understanding misled by the beliefs of others." [6]

History is continuity and advance. Traditional continuity is not mere mechanical reproduction; it is creative transformation. We must preserve the precious substance of religious reality by translating it out of the modes and thoughts of other times into terms and needs of our own day and generation. We must create common goals that will unite living faiths without permitting any feeling of dominance or inferiority. Time changes all things and the Spirit in us must guide us unto all truth.

Belief and behaviour go together. If we believe in blood, race and soil, our world will be filled with Belsens and Buchenwalds. If we behave like wild animals, our society will be a

[6] purāṇam ity eva na sādhu sarvam
na cāpi kāvyam navam ity avadyam
santaḥ parīkṣyānyatarad bhajante
mūḍhaḥ parapratyayaneya buddhiḥ. I, 2.

jungle. If we believe in universal spiritual values, peace and understanding will grow. A good tree bringeth forth good fruit. We are today concerned with fundamental issues and are eager to know the truth in its most exalted and rewarding forms.

Goethe remarks: "The one and only real and profound theme of the world and of human history—a theme to which all others are subordinate—remains the conflict between belief and unbelief. All epochs dominated by belief, in whatever shape, have a radiance and bliss of their own, and bear fruit for their people as well as for posterity. All epochs over which unbelief in whatever form maintains its miserable victory, even if they boast and shine for a while with false splendour, are ignored by posterity because nobody likes to drudge his life out over sterile things." [7] Human societies like human beings live by faith and die when faith disappears. If our society is to recover its health, it must regain its faith. Our society is not sick beyond saving for it suffers from divided loyalties, from conflicting urges, from alternating moods of exaltation and despair. This condition of anguish is our reason for hope. We need a faith which will assert the power of spirit over things and find significance in a world in which science and organisation seem to have lost their relationship to traditional values.

[7] Quoted in Erich Heller's *The Disinherited Mind* (1952), p. 77.

2

The Difficulties of Belief

AMONG the major influences which have created the problem of unbelief today are the growing scientific outlook, an awakened social conscience and interest in world unity. No religion can hope to survive if it does not satisfy the scientific temper of our age, sympathise with its social aspirations and foster the unity of the world.

I. RELIGION AND SCIENCE

The scientific temper with its restless intellectual questioning, its reluctance to accept anything on trust, its capacity to doubt has been the spur to all adventure and experiment. It does not accept any view without scrutiny or criticism and is free to ask questions and doubt assertions. This spirit has given us an amazing mastery over the material environment.

Religion, as it is generally understood, is opposed to the spirit of science. The method of science is empirical while that of religion is dogmatic. Science does not rely on authority but appeals to communicable evidence that any trained mind can evaluate. Science does not admit any barriers to freedom of thought and inquiry. It welcomes new knowledge and new experience. A true scientist does not take refuge in dogmatism. His outlook is marked by modesty, self-criticism and readiness to learn from others. If we esteem freedom of inquiry, we find that it is incompatible with authoritarianism, which is the dominant feature of religion.

Tertullian denounced all philosophy as devilish. He asked: "Where is there any likeness between the Christian and the philosopher—between the disciple of Greece and the disciple of Heaven—between one who corrupts the Truth and one who restores and teaches it?" [1] This view of the opposition between religion and reason is not altogether outmoded. "To demand a rational argument for Faith is to make Reason, that is Man, the standard of reference for faith," says Dr. H. Kraemer. [2]

For science, all judgments are provisional and subject to revision in the light of fresh knowledge. If established religions become rigid, closed and confined narrowly to a world whose boundaries are marked out in the scriptures written centuries

[1] *Apology,* XLVI. When, at the beginning of the seventeenth century, Copernicus dethroned the earth from its pre-eminence, Luther was profoundly shocked. He said, "People give ear to an upstart astrologer who strove to show that the earth revolves, not the heaven or the firmament, the sun and the moon. Whoever wishes to appear clever must devise some new system, which of all systems is, of course, the very best. This fool wishes to reverse the entire science of astronomy: but sacred scripture tells us that Joshua commanded the sun to stand still, and not the earth." Calvin similarly demolished Copernicus with the text: "The world also is stablished, that it cannot be moved," and exclaimed "who will venture to place the authority of Copernicus above that of the Holy Spirit?"
Kircher invited a Jesuit Professor to look through his telescope at the newly discovered spots in the sun; the Professor replied: "My son, it is useless. I have read Aristotle through twice and have not found anything about spots on the sun. There are no spots on the sun."
[2] *The Christian Message in a Non-Christian World* (1938), p. 106. Dr. A. Comfort writing in *Christian News-Letter* (No. 139, January 19, 1949) says: "While science has (of late) become less dogmatic, religion has come to rely increasingly on mere assertion and rarely takes the trouble to argue."

ago, those attracted by the scientific method, which has demonstrated its validity, not only theoretically but practically, through the spectacular technological results, are inclined to prefer the laboratory to the altar.

Besides, there is an element of universality about scientific views, which is not to be found in religious doctrines. Scientists recognise no national or geographical boundaries. They exchange information with fellow workers in other lands. Secrecy is repugnant to the spirit of science.

Each religion claims that its scripture is, in a unique sense, the word of God and so infallible. The inerrancy of the scriptures is inconsistent with the spirit of science. Literal infallibility is not now insisted on except by a few fundamentalists. The scriptures give us the impact of the revelation on the fallible minds and hearts of those who respond to or receive the revelation. Their utterances cannot be regarded as infallible.[3]

Many of the scriptural texts are not to be taken literally. For example, the chronology of Genesis, its account of creation as a series of abrupt and successive acts, the doctrine of the solid heaven and the stationary earth, if they are taken literally, are found to be at variance with the findings of science. Yet no religion can survive the discovery that it is rooted in beliefs which have no historical basis or spiritual reality. To divest religion of dogma, tradition and myth is to make it empty. Therefore religious authorities condemn all attempts which result in undermining belief in scriptures.[4]

[3] Professor C. H. Dodd observes: "Religious belief is, even more than scientific propositions, subject to relativity. The religious man, like the man of science, should be aware that the best statement he can make to himself is nothing more than a very inadequate symbol of ultimate reality." *The Authority of the Bible* (1928), p. 20.
[4] When the Roman Emperors granted toleration to the Christian re-

2. COMPARATIVE RELIGION

Studies in comparative religion reveal to us not only the bewildering variety of religious beliefs and practices but also the many points of resemblance between religious systems which treat themselves as opposed to each other.[5] Some of the most significant features, like incarnation, miracles and festivals, are

ligion, the Roman Catholic Church organized a system of censorship and the first book to be formally banned was *Thalia* by the priest Arius, who was judged heretical at the Council of Nicaea in A.D. 325. This system flourished throughout the Middle Ages. Soon after the invention of printing, Pope Innocent VIII, in 1467, ordered all books to be examined by the Church authorities before publication. After the Reformation, the Council of Trent (1545–1563) had a general catalogue of forbidden books. Ernest Renan sharply differentiated between the Christ and the Church which he described as a religious institution without the religious spirit. In his inaugural lecture at the *Collège de France* in 1862, he called Jesus "an incomparable man—so great that . . . I should not like to contradict those who, struck by the exceptional quality of his achievement, call him God." The orthodox were not reconciled to these revised versions of the Holy Scriptures. In a consistorial allocution of June, 1862, Pope Pius IX warned the assembled prelates of "scheming liars [who tried to] extinguish all ideas of justice, truth, right, honesty and religion. [These peddlers of] pestilential errors, . . . dare to assert that the prophecies and miracles told and explained in the Holy Scriptures are the comments of poets, and that the sacrosanct mysteries of our divine faith are mere inventions; that the two Holy Testaments are full of unfounded stories, and even that our Lord Jesus Christ, horrible to say, is a mythical fiction." *Pii IX. Pontificis Maximi Acta* (1864), *Pars Prima*, III, 453–4, quoted in the *Journal of Modern History* (December, 1953), p. 382. Renan's *Life of Jesus* was put on the Index on August 24, 1863. The present censorship policy of the Church is set forth in the Code of Canon Law introduced in 1918. All books defending atheism, materialism, divorce, duelling, suicide, abortion, contraception are banned.

[5] In the teaching of Jesus we find many parallels to that of other religions. Sir E. Hoskyns writes: "The attempts of Christian scholars to find new ethical or moral standards in Jesus have completely broken down. Jewish scholars have shown that there is no single moral aphorism recorded as spoken by Jesus which cannot be paralleled in Rabbinical literature." *The Riddle of the New Testament* (1931), p. 169. For parallels between the teachings of the Buddha and Jesus, see *Eastern Religions and Western Thought* (1939), pp. 173 ff.

found in common. The festival celebrating the renewal of life in the spring is found in many religions. It is an occasion for prayer and praise, for thanksgiving. We lift up our eyes and our hearts to the hills whence come our hope and faith, our strength and joy. The Hindus celebrate it as the Holi festival. The Jews call it the feast of Passover, the deliverance from bondage, the divine dispensation of mercy. For the Christians, it is the Holy Easter symbolic of the resurrection of Jesus and his triumph over death. The spring festival commemorates the great renewal not only in the physical but also in the spiritual world. The Greek legends of redeemer-gods have some affinity to the crucified and risen Jesus. The old paganism of the Roman Empire affected the life and thought of the Christian Church in many ways. Some of the pagan deities were canonised in the Church's Calendar of Saints under slightly changed names. Quirinus becomes "St. Quirino" of Siena, Perun, the god of lightning, "St. Elijah," Volus, the god of flocks, "St. Brasius." [6]

The Mother and Child among the gentle cattle in the stable at Bethlehem are known to India in Yaśoda and Kṛṣṇa with the cattle at Gokulam. The Queen of Heaven who was the Virgin Mother, who is adored as Mary, was known previously as Ishtar, Astoreth, Isis, Cybele, Britomartis. The travail of Christ for the salvation of mankind is foreshadowed in the labours of Gilgamesh, Herakles, Prometheus and the account of the suffering servant of Isaiah. The worship of divinity in human form is known to pre-Christians even in Rome.[7] The

[6] Edwyn Bevan writes: "There seems no doubt that the Church did borrow from Mithraism in the fixing of Christmas day on December 25th, the birthday of the Sun." *Christianity in the Light of Modern Knowledge* (1929), p. 103.
[7] "In Divus Augustus the potential converts of the first Christian missionaries had already acknowledged an incarnation of the Godhead in a

very name *Ecclesia* for the Christian Church is the technical term employed in the city-state of Athens to denote the assembly of the citizen body, when it met to transact political as distinct from judicial business. It now means a local Christian community as well as the Church universal.

When Christian theologians found many affinities and similarities between Christian and other religions, some of them imagined that they were the devices of the devil to ensnare men while the more sensible treated them as *praeparatio evangelica* for Christianity.

3. THE HUMAN INDIVIDUAL AND THE DEVELOPMENT OF TECHNOLOGY

We have grown up in a climate which persuades us to accept the criterion of reality which science has provided us. Researches in biology, psychology and history suggest that man is a creature of reflexes, at the mercy of the forces of the environment and capable of being shaped and controlled by applied sciences. To the Psalmist's question, "What is man that thou art mindful of him," mid-twentieth-century science answers that man is an animated machine or at best an animal. The biological view of man set forth in Aristotle's *De Anima* was supplemented by the ideal of the theoretical life in his *Ethics*. The religious view which insists on treating man, as, at least in some degree, free, autonomous, purposive and rational,

---

living human being whose mortal mother was fabled to have been got with child by an immortal sire, and this divine deed, which must shock the sensibilities of a philosophic soul as a vulgar moral transgression when it was attributed to an Olympian, was to shine in the self-revelation of a God, whose power was love and whose Godhead was as wholly present in the Son as in the Father—as a voluntary evacuation of His own Divinity which was a supreme act of self-sacrifice for the redemption of His fallen creatures." Arnold J. Toynbee: *A Study of History,* Vol. VII (1954), p. 458.

C

cannot be established by the controlled experiments in the laboratory. These latter do not deal with the modes in which man is aware of himself as a conscious subject.

Thanks to technology, new forms of economic organisation have come into being in which the individual is losing his sense of uniqueness and of unity with others. Our society is fast becoming one of vast organisations and diminishing personal relationships. The influence of the family, the village group, the local authority, the temple, the church or the mosque is waning. The people are restless, volatile, seldom in repose. Those who are immersed in the facilities which technical progress has put at our disposal find it difficult to make the effort for self-mastery. The more we depend on the gadgets which enable us to lead a life of comfort at the material level, the more estranged do we become from ourselves.

Like the machines which delight and enthrall them, the masses are neither good nor bad. Machines have made our lives complicated and intellect has made our minds restless. Poise, assurance and serenity seem to be beyond our grasp, and to gain a false sense of security the individual blends with others in a new entity, the mass. The spectre of the mass hovers over public affairs, industry, business, social life and manners. The great danger with the mass is not right thought or wrong thought but the utter absence of thought. The immense impact of mass media on our lives encourages passivity, acquiescence, conformity. The mind is benumbed and the will paralysed. Instead of courageous independent thinking, there is a susceptibility to words, to symbols of crude emotion. The collective wisdom of the masses is a misnomer for surrender to emotionalism. Those who manipulate the people acquire great influence. Politics has become a gamble in mass psychology.

It was the masses that stoned the Bastille; it was the masses that responded by collective rapture to Hitler-in-the-brewery. It is the masses who are being exploited today for ideological crusades. The leaders of public opinion use the techniques of propaganda for controlling public opinion. If we listen to the radio or follow the television programme, we will see how the masses decide a nation's foreign policy, a scientist's moral fibre, an artist's creativity and an automobile's quality.

In a technological civilisation, in a mass society, the individual becomes a depersonalised unit. Things control life. Statistical averages replace qualitative human beings. To be human is to be trusting, to be kind, to be co-operative, to be sympathetic and responsive. It is to be democratic and not be afraid to exchange opinions even with those who differ from us. It is to trust our neighbours and be magnanimous to our enemies. If we recover our humanity we will refuse to submit to arbitrary authority and help nations to recover from the state of collective paranoia into which some of them have fallen. But the technological organisation of modern society in which the individual counts for less and less fosters a funda-mental scepticism and negation of the spirit of man.

Modern governments tend to attack and destroy the self-respect in human beings. Little by little they transform human beings into mere objects, conscious of themselves as such and forced in the end to despair of themselves. This happens not merely at the intellectual level but in the very depths of the soul. These are the people who have lost their souls, *ātmahano janāh* as the Upanisad says. Self-possession, *ātmalābha,* is to have faith in the inner tribunal of conscience, a tribunal un-violated and indeed inviolable by any intrusion of external power, an inalienable inner sovereignty, an absolute possession of the self by the self. There is in us a level of being, an order of reality, a spark of spirit. We do not belong entirely to the world of objects to which modern scientific techniques are seeking to assimilate us. Between the possible use of the atomic weapons and the degradation of man there is a secret bond.[8] If we are to retain our moral integrity, technical progress has to be balanced by increased self-mastery.

4. LOGICAL EMPIRICISM

Empiricism has been a persistent feature of philosophy, both in the East and in the West. Till recently it connoted a definite theory of human knowledge based on sensation and inference, a contempt for metaphysical abstractions, a reverence for scientific method, a system of ethics which is humanist in character and an agnosticism in religion. These empiricists possessed a world outlook and adopted a definite attitude to life and thought. They may be said to be philosophers in the traditional sense of the term, with definite views on the nature of the individual, his place in the world and his destiny.

The new empiricists repudiate all metaphysics. Nothing that is not evident to the senses or to the extension of the senses provided by scientific instruments has any claim to truth. The world of matter that science explores is real and everything else that is real must be of the same nature as matter. Matter

---

[8] Trajan in Virgil Gheorgious' *The Twenty-Fifth Hour* (1950), says: "In the most recent phase of its development, Western civilisation is no longer taking account of the individual and there seem no grounds for hoping that it will ever do so again. That society knows only a few of the dimensions of the individual, man in his wholeness considered as an individual no longer exists for it. The West has created a society which resembles a machine. It forces men to live in the heart of this society and to adapt themselves to the laws of the machine. When men come to resemble machines sufficiently to identify themselves with machines, then there will be no more men on the face of the earth."

is all that we can see and touch. Whatever is capable of empirical verification is true. To apprehend values, to enjoy beauty is irrelevant to the question of truth. It is to wander in a world of unrealities, of shadows, of illusions. An unseen spiritual reality is an unnecessary intruder in the vast impersonal process of space-time.

Francis Bacon said: "All the received philosophical systems are but so many stage plays, representing worlds of their own creation after an unreal and scenic fashion. Nor is it only of the systems now in vogue, or of the ancient sects and philosophies that I speak: for many more plays of the same kind may yet be composed and in like artificial manner set forth." [9] Here Bacon contrasts philosophic speculations with trustworthy scientific generalisations. Hume, in the same spirit, remarks: "Here indeed lies the justest and most plausible objection against a considerable part of metaphysics that they are not properly a science; but arise either from the fruitless efforts of human vanity, which would penetrate into subjects utterly inaccessible to the understanding, or from the craft of popular superstitions which, being unable to depend themselves on fair ground, raise these entangling brambles to cover and protect their weakness." [10]

And in his *Treatise on Human Nature* he affirms that evaluating attitudes have no theoretical content. They are original data which prove nothing beyond themselves. They are not cognitive in character. They do not say anything about matters of fact. Meaningful statements are limited to empirical facts and tautologies. So many questions we raise about the nature of the universe are couched in language which

[9] *Novum Organum.*
[10] *Enquiries Concerning Human Understanding,* Section I.

makes them meaningless. Emotional experiences of value do not convey information about matters of fact. They are not derived from facts or founded on them.

If all knowledge is derived from experience, Kant asked, what is the status of *synthetic judgments a priori?* They are neither relations of ideas nor matters of fact. Hume's scepticism did not satisfy Kant, who argued that the external world is a construction of the imagination from the manifold of changing impressions. It is impossible for us to know any reality independent of experience. Mathematical propositions are neither analytic truths of logic, nor synthetic propositions subject to confirmation in experience. Yet these propositions which are neither tautologies nor empirical generalisations are necessarily true.

A. N. Whitehead and Bertrand Russell in their *Principia Mathematica* tried to show that the propositions of mathematics have essentially the same type of generality as the propositions of logic. Both these are independent of any subject matter or reference to objects of experience. Mathematics and logic should be regarded as continuous with each other since they both deal with the formal properties of symbolic systems. Aristotelian logic is not purely formal. It takes into account particular grammatical forms and types of inference based on them. The strictly formal part of logic is of the same character as mathematics, while the part of logic that deals with the implications of the various and necessary forms of language is a different discipline.

Following Hume, G. E. Moore looks upon philosophy as purely descriptive and not creative or constructive. It is more a method than a doctrine. According to Hume, philosophical theories which attempt more than description rest on confu-

sions arising from the working of the human mind. Moore
thinks that they are all traceable to the use of language. So
when any philosophical theory is suggested, Moore insists that
we should try to know what exactly it means. It is not for
philosophy to formulate theories of morality and religion or
even decide between conflicting views of them. Its task is to
show that these theories are without any content, nonsensical,
empty words.

The function of philosophy is analysis, clarification. Like
any form of inquiry, its method is empirical, experimental,
analytic. Its function is to define as clearly as possible the limits
of human knowledge and set down the distinctions between
different kinds of knowledge. Philosophy should cease to concern itself with the central problems arising from the human
situation and concentrate on the formal analysis of semantic
conundrums.

We now seem to live in a period of scientific self-sufficiency
when we dismiss ultimate questions as absurd and unanswer-
able, when we look upon human beings as complicated
machines and disregard their agonies and ecstasies as survivals
of a prescientific age. We pretend that the world we comprehend in sterilised sobriety is the only world there is. Religion
is being slowly edged out of existence.

5. RELIGION AND SOCIAL RELATIONS

The inadequacy of religion is evident from the disparity
between outward allegiance and inward betrayal. Religion is
confused with the mechanical participation in the rites or
passive acquiescence in the dogmas. Many of those who observe the forms of religion, the gestures of faith, the conven-
tions of piety do not model their lives on the precepts they

profess. We keep up the forms of religion, which seem to be of the nature of play-acting.[11]

Religions, at their best, insist on behaviour more than on belief. Orthodoxy is not confined to the defining of faith. It includes the living of it. Definition is the means and not the end. A vehicle is not more important than the goal to which it is to take us. We must live religion in truth and deed and not merely profess it in words. There is a difference today between our belief and our behaviour. And yet we say that "faith without works is dead." [12] St. Paul says: "Do not be conformed to this world but be transformed by the renewal of your mind, that you may prove what is the will of God, what is good and acceptable and perfect." [13] If religion is not dynamic and pervasive, if it does not penetrate every form of human life and influence every type of human activity, it is only a veneer and not a reality. If, on the other hand, we believe that our faith is widespread and its adherents are conforming their acts to the ideals they profess, then the conclusion is inevitable that religion is invaluable as a means for the improvement of the individual and society.

[11] Canon Sydney Smith wrote in the *Edinburgh Review:* "If the Bible is diffused in Hindustan, what must be the astonishment of the natives, to find that we are forbidden to rob, murder and steal; *we,* who in fifty years, have extended our Empire over the whole [Indian] peninsula, and exemplified in our public conduct every crime of which human nature is capable. What matchless impudence, to follow up such *practice* with such *precepts.*" April, 1809, p. 45.

S. T. Coleridge affirmed his "strong conviction that the conversion of a single province of Christendom to true and practical Christianity would do more towards the conversion of heathenism than an army of missionaries." *Notes on English Divines* (1853), Vol. II, p. 67. He felt that it would be wiser to check the heathenism at home before trying to remove it abroad.

[12] James 2:17.

[13] Romans 12:2.

Thanks to science, amenities of living have greatly increased. In regard to all these scientific conveniences, religions have been hostile. When anaesthetics were used to relieve women of pain in childbirth, it was argued that God had intended women to suffer; otherwise he would not have made childbirth painful. To mitigate women's labour pains is to thwart God's intentions and is therefore impious.

The cult of suffering for its own sake has nothing in common with the main tradition of Hindu and Greek thought. Christianity hardens the dualism between man and nature. To save one's soul, one must resist the failings of the flesh and their seductive images. The puritanism of religions condemns all pleasures unless they are joined to the fear of God. Human learning and art, poetry and painting, music and literature are said to be the snares of the devil.

There are some who seek escape from the troubles of the world on the comfortable assumption that spiritual life is different from the ordinary social life. They take flight into a spiritual esotericism which retreats from life. Estranged from the concrete tasks of knowledge and of action, these deserters from life retreat into a beyond of an aesthetic-contemplative life in the belief that religion is primarily concerned with another order of existence and the good it seeks is not "of this world." These exiles from life slip away from urgent human tasks to the shelter of a protected existence. By setting up a gulf between the sacred and the secular, by developing an insensitiveness to the tragic fate of the world, by withdrawing from the scene of mankind's social agony, by proclaiming that justice can be found only beyond the grave, religion is robbed of the possibility of social regeneration.

We cannot draw a sharp line of distinction between religion

and social life. Social organisation rests ultimately on a series
of decisions taken by human beings as to the manner in which
they and their followers shall live. These decisions are matters
of spiritual discernment while actions to implement them require technical knowledge and social sense.

It is true that religion is not a social reform movement and
yet a large part of one's life is spent in society. A stable social
order is the ground work of civilised life. Religion is a social
cement, a way in which men express their aspirations and find
solace for their frustrations.

If we do not interpret religion as a way of escape, we seek
to make it a defence of the established order. All religions are
conformist in spirit and try to appease those who hold power
in the world. They even lean on them for support. The spirit
of conformity and appeasement are not the monopoly of any
one religion. There are some Hindus even today—happily
their number is diminishing—who are the frightened defenders
of caste and untouchability which are an offence and a scan-
dal. Christianity has no doubt been responsible for abolishing
slavery and righting many social wrongs, but as a community,
the Christians do not profess to live up to the precepts of the
Gospels. They do not see the beam in their own eye, or take
up the cross and drink the cup.

Even the founders of religions accept the sufferings of the
major part of humanity as part of their necessary lot in life, if
not a penance for some heavy guilt which they have incurred
in their previous lives. They promise future happiness for their
present suffering and conjure up visions of paradise to redress
the balance, to soothe the suffering and the revolt of tortured
men. So social idealists condemn religion as "dope" artificially
administered as a soporific, a device adopted by those who do

not themselves take it seriously though they expect others to do so. Religion is condemned as an imposture kept alive by its alliance with vested interests.

In the eyes of God all men are equal. No one acknowledged this lesson more freely and more knowingly than the framers of the American Constitution. We are familiar with the ringing words of Jefferson in the Declaration of Independence: ". . . that all men are created equal, that they are endowed by their Creator with certain unalienable Rights, that among these are Life, Liberty and the pursuit of Happiness." These words are not mere phrases of propaganda but the products of a deep-felt faith. In the last letter which Jefferson ever wrote, he commented on the meaning of this declaration. "The mass of mankind was not born with saddles on their backs, nor a favoured few booted and spurred, ready to ride them legitimately, by the grace of God." Even today we are not prepared to treat all men as equals. Our deeds do not match our words.

The capitalist system of society does not foster healthy relations among human beings. When a few people own all the means of production, the others, though they may be nominally free in the sense that they are neither slaves nor serfs, have to sell their labour under conditions imposed on them. The emphasis of capitalism on the supreme importance of material wealth, the intensity of its appeal to the acquisitive instincts, its worship of economic power, often with little regard to the ends which power serves or the means which it uses, its support of property in general, not merely particular rights of property, its subordination of human beings to the exigencies of an economic system, its exploitation of them to the limits of endurance, its concentration on the largest profit rather than on maximum production, its acceptance of divisions in the human family based on differences, not of personal quality and social function but of income and economic circumstance, all these are injurious to human dignity. So long as the capitalist society encourages these concepts and habits, it subsidises social unrest.

In the East especially, the present distribution of power and opportunity, where a few have a chance of living without working while the large majority have their backs broken by the burdens they bear, cries out for redress. But the silence and uncertainty of religious teachers in regard to social problems such as slums and unemployment, their indifference to the common people who are depressed by hunger and weakened by artificial divisions have lowered the prestige of religion. Social movements which attempt to implement principles and equality are condemned by the official spokesmen of religions.[14]

Racial discrimination is opposed to the teaching of world brotherhood.[15] The world judges us not by our precept but by our example.

All religions insist on compassion to the suffering. Christianity, for example, asks us to do good to them that hate us and despitefully use us. There is nothing special in loving those who love us or who are themselves lovable. Jesus asks us to love our enemies in the hope of reawakening their humanness,

[14] In 1864 Pope Pius IX issued the encyclical *Quanta Cura* in which he condemned as "pests, socialism, communism, Bible Societies, and Clerico-Liberal Societies." Eng. translation (1875), p. 15. In 1891 Pope Leo XIII, in his encyclical *De Rerum Novarum* denounced socialism as robbery and demanded that its tenets be "utterly rejected by all Catholics." Eng. translation (1891), pp. 7, 13. The official attitude of the Roman Catholic Church to socialism and communism continues the same.

[15] Dr. J. C. Carothers, in his Report on the psychology of Mau Mau, urged Europeans in Kenya to live truly Christian lives if they wish their teachings to have a lasting effect on the African population. "If the general white population of this colony" he states, "cannot practise Christian principles in their dealings with their fellow-men, both white and black, the missionaries might just as well pack up their bags and go."

their potential capacity for love. We are called upon to remove from the enemy's heart the fear of our own hateful intentions. How far do we carry out these instructions to be good even to those who hate us?

Religious leaders are generally silent about the satanic crimes of modern warfare. They use equivocation and sophistry to defend them. The late Mr. F. D. Roosevelt declared on September 1, 1939: "The ruthless bombing from the air of civilians in unfortified centres of population during the course of hostilities which have raged in various quarters of the earth in the past few years, which have resulted in the maiming and death of thousands of defenceless women and children, has profoundly shocked the conscience of humanity." His successor, Mr. Truman, sanctioned the use of the first uranium bomb, which fell on the Japanese seaport of Hiroshima on August 6, 1945. In using these weapons, man has set aside God and listened to the voice of the serpent: "Ye shall be as gods." After Hiroshima, a Jesuit missionary in Japan vainly appealed to Rome for a ruling. On the 6th of June, 1954, the Archdeacon of London, speaking from the pulpit of St. Paul's Cathedral, assured the Christian world that the Christian faith lent no countenance to that pacifism which "would suffer the blotting out of civilisation or the enslavement of whole countries." [16] It is not beyond the ingenuity of our religious spokesmen to use equivocation and sophistry to defend what the states wish to do. [17]

---

[16] Two days later on the 8th of June, General Gruenther, speaking in London, said: "We have one asset now which is of tremendous value. We have a long-range aircraft to which the Soviet now have no answer. I refer to the plane B-47, which can fly so fast and so high that there is no defence against it in this year of 1954."

[17] In 1929, after the *Concordat* between Mussolini and the Holy See, the Pope saluted Il Duce as a "man of God" and in 1932 he gave him

Forty years ago Bernard Shaw wrote in *Common Sense About the War:*

> We turn our Temples of Peace promptly into Temples of War, and exhibit our parsons as the most pugnacious characters in the community. I venture to affirm that the sense of scandal given by this is far deeper and more general than the Church thinks, especially among the working classes, who are apt either to take religion seriously or else to repudiate it and criticise it closely. When a bishop, at the first shot, abandons the worship of Christ and rallies his flock round the altar of Mars, he may be acting patriotically, necessarily, manfully, rightly; but that does not justify him in pretending that there has been no change, and that Christ is, in effect, Mars. The straightforward course, and the one that would serve the Church best in the long run, would be to close our professedly Christian Churches the moment war is declared by us, and reopen them only on the signing of the treaty of peace.

We conceal from ourselves the true nature of what we do by euphemisms. If we strip away all pretence and are honest with ourselves, we will know that we are fast losing faith in decency. A deep qualitative change for the worse is taking place in the public mind.

---

the Papal blessing at St. Peter's. Four years later, the Italian clergy were ordered to celebrate the Fascist victory over Ethiopia with special services for thanksgiving in the churches. In the same year (1936) in the Spanish Civil War, the Pope anathematised the Republican forces as satanic, and blessed the armies of General Franco, who decorated his guns with the emblem of the Sacred Heart of Jesus! The present Pope, whose penetration of mind and love of humanity are well known, I am sure, would not support such measures.

When racial inequalities are condemned, the supporters of separate churches for the white and the coloured peoples in South Africa and the Southern States of the United States appeal to the Biblical curse pronounced on Ham and his descendants. Genesis 9:22–25.

In totalitarian systems of politics and religion, policies and practices are defended or condemned, not in terms of their probable consequences in real life but for their correctness or incorrectness as interpretations of the appropriate sacred books. Intelligent men devote their brains to discussions about the number of angels that can stand upon the point of a needle or to debates whether a particular country's socialism is strictly Marxist and not whether it is true. In our allegiance to dogmas, we overlook the claims of truth and the happiness of men. When questions of the abolition of *sati* arose in India, the fundamentalists turned to scriptures and quoted texts and did not concern themselves about human life and misery. Such things are possible only when faith in God dies out and niceties of ritual and the logic of dogmas alone matter. Our conscience is anaesthetised by dogmas.

For the spread of religious scepticism, historical religions have to bear a heavy measure of responsibility. In spite of the great contributions religions, through the ages, have made for the promotion of art, culture and spiritual life, they have been vitiated by dogmatism and fanaticism, by cruelty and intolerance and by the intellectual dishonesty of their adherents. So long as religions adapt their principles to the ruling interests of this world, so long as they support the established order however iniquitous it may be, those who revolt against such practises are the truly religious people. Bakunin in his book *God and the State* urges that the state find its principal support in the idea of God, which is the rejection of human reason, of justice and of freedom. He calls for a social revolution, which is "the one thing that will get the power to shut all the pubs and all the churches at the same time."

The atheist may be a poor specimen but not more than the

pharisee. The Romans, said Polybius, were more religious than the gods themselves. We deem ourselves religious even when we plan deliberately the destruction of innocent millions. No religion has a claim to our allegiance if it does not produce a tradition of humanity and social responsibility.

6. RELIGION AND WORLD UNITY

We cannot build a society of nations by fostering economic and political ties alone. We have to give to the new society a psychological unity, a spiritual coherence. To sustain a world community, we need unity, if not identity of spiritual outlook and aspiration. Unfortunately religions tend to keep people apart. Humanity is broken up into a number of separate worlds each with its particular religious tradition.

The root meaning of the word "religion" suggests that it should be a binding force, and yet by their claims to finality and absoluteness, the attitude of religions to one another is one of unmitigated hostility. The Old Testament view illustrates this spirit. The war cry of Moses, as he led the children of Israel, was: "Rise up, Yahveh! Let thine enemies be scattered!" [18] Yahveh was the God of the Hebrews, always at war with other gods. Deuteronomy records: "When Yahveh, your God, puts them [the heathen] into your hands, you must exterminate them, making no compact with them, and showing no mercy. . . . Demolish their altars, break their obelisks, cut down their sacred poles and burn up their idols!" [19] The intolerance of the Hebrews to other religions was based on the view that their God was one of righteousness and truth while others were devoid of any ethical qualities. They believed in the existence of other gods though they were confident that

[18] Numbers 10:35.
[19] 7:2–5.

their God was the greatest of them all: "There is none like unto thee among the gods, O Lord." [20] The prophet Micah (8th century B.C.) had an idea of the peaceful coexistence of different gods. He suggests that other gods had legitimate claims on the loyalty of their own peoples. "All nations may live loyal each to its own god; but we will live ever loyal to our god, Yahveh." [21]

When monotheism developed Yahveh became the one and only God. "I am Yahveh, the maker of all things; I alone stretched out the heavens; I spread out the earth; Who aided me? I am Yahveh; there is no God besides me." [22] Though the Hebrews were convinced that they were the only people who had received a true revelation from God, they had a conception of the universality of God. Other people were also the objects of God's care. "What are you more than the Ethiopians, O Israelites?" asks Yahveh. "I brought up Israel from Egypt—yes, and Philistines from Crete, from Kir the Armenians." [23] If we admit the universal fatherhood of God, we cannot believe that he is fatherly only to those who believe in this or that God and is a God of intolerable wrath to others. Worshippers of other gods were treated kindly because they were potential recruits to the Temple of Yahveh which will become a "house of prayer for every nation." [24] Yet the Old Testament is dominated by the status of Israel as God's chosen people. The apocalypse of Ezra dismisses all non-Jews as worthless.[25]

[20] Psalm 86.
[21] Micah 4:5.
[22] Isaiah 44:24.
[23] Amos 9:7.
[24] Isaiah 56:7.
[25] "O Lord, thou hast said that for our [the Jews'] sakes, thou madest the world. As for the other nations, thou hast said that they are nothing and like unto spittle." II Esdras 6:55 ff.

D

The conception of being the chosen people, which is not peculiar to the Jews, results in practices and attitudes which emphasise the notions of superiority and exclusiveness. It does not foster a sympathetic understanding of other great religious traditions but encourages hostile isolation. The best of us do not have a clean slate to write on. We do not live in a vacuum. Jesus was trained in the exclusivist atmosphere of the Hebrews, though he struggled hard to overcome it. The Hebrew tradition provided Jesus with the idiom and thought forms in which his mind developed. He spoke as a Jew, as a child of Israel. In the story of the heathen woman of Tyre and Sidon, Jesus refuses her cry for help: "Let the children first be filled, for it is not fair to take the children's bread and throw it to the dogs." [26] In Matthew, his reply is more decisive: "I was not sent to any except the lost sheep of the house of Israel." [27] He is recorded as saying: "No man cometh unto the Father but by Me." [28] This view is emphasised in the Apostolic preaching. "In none other name is there salvation, for neither is there any other name under heaven, given among men, whereby we must be saved." [29] While the Jews and the Muslims agree that Jesus was a prophet, they would not suffer him to take precedence over Moses and Muhammad.

The Jewish background of Christianity gave to it an exclusive regionalism and a hostility to Hellenistic influence. The religious literature and sacred history derived by Christianity from Judaism are totally different in spirit from the classical tradition. In the Apostolic period Judaic influence diminished. Christianity as a world religion was born not in Judaea but in

[26] Mark 7:24–30.
[27] 15:24.
[28] John 14:6; see also Matthew 11:27; Luke 10:22.
[29] Acts 4:12.

the great cities of the Mediterranean world, Antioch and Ephesus, Thessalonica and Corinth, Rome and Alexandria. Greek culture arose in those parts of the Mediterranean world where the Greeks came into contact with the civilisations of the East. The fusion between the particularism of Judaea and the universalism of Greece is still unresolved and many modern theologians still emphasise the special and exclusive character of the Christian religion.

Emil Brunner says: "The unique and unrepeatable character of revelation constitutes the essence of Christianity. A final event can only happen once." [30] Karl Barth says: "God has revealed himself to man in Jesus Christ. What do we know from any other source of God? . . Absolutely nothing." [31] One's own religion is contrasted with other religions as truth against falsehood. It is a question of either—or. It is either light or darkness. In a recent Anglican book, the primary purpose of the Christian missionary is said to be "to abolish all other religions of the world." [32] Dr. Julius Richter of the University of Berlin wrote in 1913: "wherever missionary enterprise comes into contact with non-Christian religions, it sets itself to oust them and to put Christianity in their place." [33] Dr. Schlink, Professor of Missions in Tübingen, writes: "On one side stand God's words and acts, on the other the daemonic impulse to picture God in one's own image. . . . Any attempt to make links with them would be to make links with lies and deception." [34] The claims to truth and finality are put forward

[30] *The Mediator,* Eng. translation (1934), pp. 25ff.
[31] *The Knowledge of God* (1937–38), p. 43.
[32] C. J. Shebbeare, *Christianity and Other Religions* (1939), p. 13.
[33] *International Review of Missions* (July, 1913), p. 522.
[34] *Ibid.* (July, 1938), pp. 465, 470.

on behalf of the sects of Christianity also,[35] Protestant and
Catholic, Anglican and Puritan. Nestorius of Antioch told
Theosodius: "Give me, O Caesar, give me the earth purged of
heretics and I will give you in exchange the Kingdom of
Heaven. Exterminate with me the heretics, and with you I will
exterminate the Persians." [36] Protestants and Catholics are
hostile to each other. Luther included the Roman Church
within heathendom: "Those who are outside Christianity, be
they heathens, Turks, Jews or false Christians [i.e., Roman
Catholics], although they may believe in only one true God,
yet remain in eternal wrath and perdition." [37] John Knox, in
his *Godly Letter to the Faithful in London* (1554), wrote:
"What is in Asia? Ignorance of God. What is in Africa? Abnegation of the Veric Saviour, our Lord Jesus. What is in the
Churches of the Grecianis? Mohamet and his false sect? What

[35] Cf. Dr. Sergius Bulgakoff: "There is only one true Church, the
Orthodox Church." "The Church, Truth and infallibility are synony-
mous." *The Orthodox Church* (1935), pp. 104–79. Mr. Douglas Jerrold
says of the Roman Catholic Church: "Christian civilisation was the
work, as the Christians must believe, of a teaching Church founded by
Almighty God himself, a Church, which, according to his promise, was
to be inspired and guided by him and preserved against error until the
end of the world." He continues: "Western civilisation has at its heart
something which no other civilisation has had—the knowledge of God's
purposes for man in this world, and of the means whereby in correspondence with divine grace man can cooperate with God's purposes and save
his soul." *Times Literary Supplement* (May 14, 1954), p. 345. S. T.
Coleridge's words on sectarian disputes are well known: "He who begins
by loving Christianity better than truth will proceed by loving his own
sect or Church better than Christianity and end in loving himself better
than all."
[36] Gibbon, *The Decline and Fall of the Roman Empire,* Chap.
XLVII. Nestorius himself was later condemned as a heretic and Gibbon
comments: "Humanity may drop a tear on the fate of Nestorius; yet
justice must observe that he suffered the persecution which he had ap-
proved and inflicted." *Ibid.*
[37] *Larger Catechism* II, 111, Eng. translation (1896), p. 106.

is in Rome?—The greatest ydoll of all uthers, that man of syn!" [38] George Tyrrell observes: "Jesus would say that Harnack was 'not far from the Kingdom of God,' but that a miss is as good as a mile; that there was no difference between Protestants and savages, all would burn in hell alike." [39]

Sometimes this attitude of unconscious superiority is couched in very courteous terms. While it is maintained that the Christian revelation is *sui generis* and entirely different from other revelations, friendly co-operation among them is not ruled out. While the Christian truth is the highest, the full radiance, others are like broken lights. Christianity fulfils the partial truths that are to be found in other religions. This view does not give up the position that Christianity is the one and only perfect religion for the whole of mankind. While it encourages interreligious co-operation and even allows that one's religious knowledge may be enriched by contact with other faiths, it does not diminish in any way the confidence that Christianity is "the faith once for all delivered to the saints." If God has given to other religions some distinctive apprehensions of religious truth, it is for the purpose that they should contribute to the fulness of truth.[40]

In 1930, the Lambeth Conference affirmed, through its committee on the Christian Doctrine of God: "We gladly acknowledge the truths contained and emphasised in the great religions; but . . . each of them is less than the Gospel of the unsearchable riches of Christ. The majesty of the God in Islam, the high moral standards and profound truth in other Eastern

[38] See *International Review of Missions* (June, 1942), p. 842.
[39] M. D. Petre, *The Life of George Tyrrell* (1912), p. 400.
[40] Dr. J. N. Farquhar in his book on *The Crown of Hinduism* (1912, p. 45) affirmed: "Christ provides the fulfilment of the highest aspirations of Hinduism. . . . He is the Crown of the Faith of India."

religions, are approaches to the truth of God revealed in Christ." [41] This view is in conformity with the statement of Jesus: "Think not that I am come to destroy the Law and the Prophets; I came, not to destroy, but to fulfill." [42]

All missionary religions, Buddhism, Christianity and Islam, believe in their own superiority. They all profess that they have the highest truth. How is any one claim to be preferred to others? We fall back on faith. "It is a mistake to suppose that the unique cosmical significance that Christianity attaches to its founder can be sustained by a simple induction from the recorded events of his earthly life," says Professor A. E. Taylor.[43] When we get beyond proof and evidence to the region of faith, each one claims for his act of faith infallibility resulting in intolerance. The absolutist claims made by these faiths are from their very nature incompatible with the existence of several such faiths. By demanding loyalty to warring creeds, arbitrary and unverifiable, we turn men against one another. Our efforts to co-ordinate moral and spiritual forces to shape the future are being sterilised by the rivalries of religions.

7. THE GROWTH OF UNBELIEF

Millions of people wish to believe, but they cannot, even though these orphaned children make use of the outer framework of religions. We are christened, or baptised, married, buried or cremated according to our religious rites, but all the time we are victims of an involuntary hypocrisy. We live in an age which is numbed and disillusioned. Our values are blurred, our thought is confused and our aims are wavering. In the life of spirit which is the vital secret of all civilisation, which in-

[41] *Lambeth Report* (1930), p. 75.
[42] Matthew 5:17.
[43] *The Faith of a Moralist* (1930), p. 126.

tellect may foster and develop but cannot create or even keep alive, we are uprooted. When the roots are destroyed, a tree may continue to live and even seem to flourish for a time, but its days are numbered. T. S. Eliot in his poem "The Wasteland" describes the decomposition of modern civilisation, the lack of conviction and direction, the poverty, confusion and meaninglessness of modern consciousness. This atmosphere of negative thought is responsible for the increase of mental cases in the modern world.[44]

Writing on the 19th of July, 1891, Lord Acton said, "For 200 years, from the time of Hobbes, unbelief has been making its way. Unbelief came to be founded on science, because about one half of the classic writing, of the creative thinking of the world was done by unbelievers. The influences that reigned were in great measure atheistic. No man could be reared except by aid of Grote, Mill, Austin, Darwin, Lewis, Huxley, Tyndall—to take England only." [45] Forty-five years

[44] C. G. Jung observes: "I have treated many hundreds of patients, the large number being Protestants, a smaller number Jews and not more than five or six believing Catholics. Among all my patients in the second half of my life, there has not been one whose problem in the last resort was not that of finding a religious outlook on life. It is safe to say that every one of them fell ill because he had lost that which the living religions of every age have given their followers and none of them has really been healed who did not regain his religious outlook." *Modern Man in Search of a Soul* (1933), p. 264.

[45] *Selections from the Correspondence of the First Lord Acton,* edited by J. N. Figgis and R. V. Lawrence, Vol. II (1917). Letter dated July 19, 1891.

In the Preface to *Late Lyrics and Earlier* (1922), Thomas Hardy wrote: "Whether owing to the barbarizing of taste in the younger minds by the dark madness of the late war, the unabashed cultivation of selfishness in all classes, the plethoric growth of knowledge with the stunting of wisdom, a degrading thirst after outrageous stimulation (to quote Wordsworth) or from any other cause, we seem threatened with a new Dark Age."

after Lord Acton wrote this, T. S. Eliot declared, "The greater part of our reading matter is coming to be written by people who not only have no real belief (in a supernatural order) but are even ignorant of the fact that there are still people in the world so 'backward' or so eccentric as to continue to believe." [46] Under such guidance, religious illiteracy has been steadily increasing and civilisation is getting detached from its roots. We are face to face with a philosophy of nihilism, which is not the invention of Soviet Russia.[47]

Nietzsche does not preach a conventional atheism. He disturbs the complacency of the pharisees of unbelief and portrays European nihilism, the state of human souls and societies faced with a total eclipse of all values. He asks: "What does nihilism mean?" and answers: "It means that supreme values devalue themselves. There is no goal and no answer to our questioning." Completely disillusioned, he cries out: "Where is my home? I seek and have sought and have not found it. O eternal everywhere, O eternal nowhere? In vain." "European man,"

[46] *Essays* (1936), p. 122.

[47] In a passage of Nietzsche's *Gay Science* the whole spiritual situation from which the pronouncement of the death of God springs is described: "Have you not heard of that madman who, in the broad light of the forenoon, lit a lantern and ran into the marketplace, crying incessantly I am searching for God! . . . As it happened many were standing together there, who did not believe in God, and so he aroused great laughter. The madman leapt right among them. . . . 'Where is God?' he cried; 'Well, I will tell you. *We have murdered him,* you and I. . . . But how did we do this deed? . . . Who gave us the sponge with which to wipe out the whole horizon? What did we do when we unchained our earth from her sun? Whither is it moving now? Whither are we moving? Are we not falling incessantly? Are we not staggering through infinite nothingness? Is night not approaching and more and more night? Must we not light lanterns in the forenoon? Behold the noise of the gravediggers, busy to bury God. . . . And we have killed him! What possible comfort is there for us? Is not the greatness of the deed too great for us? To appear worthy of it, must not we ourselves become gods?' "

says Berdyaev, "stands amid a frightening emptiness. He no longer knows where the keystone of his life may be found, beneath his feet he feels no depth of solidity." [48] Nihilism is the last word of metaphysics which refuses to go beyond the surface appearances.[49] We see, on all sides, a violent loosening of the familiar bonds, a snapping of the strands that hold a civilisation together.[50]

[48] *The End of Our Time* (1933), p. 189.

[49] It is interesting to know that the Society of Philosophical Inquiry which met for fifty-seven years in the capital of the United States of America decided to close down in the year 1950 for the obvious reason of "apathy of the members toward philosophical thinking."

[50] Dr. Hensley Henson, when Bishop of Durham, wrote: "We see in our land tens of millions of men and women who acknowledge no connection with religion and, as a result of this, a large proportion of our children are growing up without religious influence or religious teaching of any sort." *Bishoprick Papers* (1946), p. 306.

Cf. Christopher Dawson: "It is clear that contemporary culture can no longer be regarded as Christian, since it is probably the most completely secularised form of culture that has ever existed." *Mediaeval Essays* (1953), p. 9.

3

The Need for Belief

LARGE sections of the people of the world today are victims of unwilling disbelief. They are not able to stand inside the cloistered walls of the traditional forms yet they require a faith, a frame of reference for their present needs and tasks. Man cannot continue for long to live in a state of disequilibrium or deprivation. What Kant says of metaphysics, that it is an instinct which we cannot destroy, however much its successful achievement may be denied, is true of religion.[1] The instinct for it may be homeless for a time but it cannot be destroyed. To live without faith is impossible. If nature has horror of a vacuum, the human soul has fear of emptiness. "Man must and will have some religion," said Blake. "If he has not the religion of Jesus, he will have the religion of Satan, and will erect the synagogue of Satan, calling the Prince of this world God and destroying all who do not worship Satan under the name of God." [2] One must believe, no matter what. To those

[1] Kant writes: "That the human mind will ever give up metaphysical researches entirely is as little to be expected as that we should prefer to give up breathing altogether to avoid inhaling impure air. There will therefore, always be metaphysics in the world, nay, every one, especially every man of reflection will have it, and for want of a recognised standard, will shape it for himself after his own pattern." Mahaffy's Eng. translation, p. 138.

[2] *Jerusalem*, pp. 52–53.

who suffer from spiritual starvation, even a rotten fruit may taste like bread from heaven; the water from a poisoned well may come as living water to those perishing of thirst. The soul knows its terrible bondage. There is no God and there must be God. Men insist on believing in something for we cannot submit to an unknown fear. The spiritual homelessness of modern man cannot last long. To belong nowhere, to be incapable of committing oneself is to be isolated. It is not ease but a personal burden. We must win back our lost security. We are prepared to pay for it any price, even that of intellectual integrity. Since the close of the seventeenth century there has been a progressive displacement of traditional religions by one form or other of man worship. Attempts to save the individual on a secular rather than a religious basis have become popular.[3]

2. RELAPSE INTO THE SUBHUMAN

Sometimes we attempt to go back into the subhuman, become unthinking, unreflective. Whether the Babylonian God seeks to put an end to the uproar of the world with the words "I want to sleep" or whether the human being wishes to relapse to the garden of Eden before he ate of the Tree of Knowledge, whether he considers it best he had never been born, whether he looks upon rational consciousness as a

---

[3] "To live not wantonly but warily—wary of a transcendental reality—is the strict meaning of the Latin word *religiosus* and indeed the essential meaning of all religion. What a man believes and what he therefore regards as unquestionable reality constitutes his religion. *Religio* does not derive from *religare,* to bind—that is, man to God. The adjective, as is often the case, has preserved the original meaning of the noun and *religiosus* stands for scrupulous, not trifling, conscientious. The opposite of religion thus would be negligence, carelessness, indifference, laxity. Over against *religo* we have *neg-lego; religens* (religiosus) is contrasted with *neglegens." Concord and Liberty* by José Ortega y Gasset (1946), p. 22.

calamity and desires to bring it to an end, we are not facing the problem but evading it. The urge to get back to the sub-human or animal life, which overtakes us in times of adversity, is illusory. Man cannot recapture his animal consciousness. Even if he refuses to employ his intellectual consciousness, he cannot get back the original integration with the environment. He cannot get rid of his memory and expectancy. Psychological evolution is irreversible in its main tendency. We cannot get away from the strains of self-consciousness by sinking into the simplicity of biological existence. We can learn from Job when he seeks his asylum in sleep: "When I say, My bed shall comfort me, my couch shall ease my complaint, then thou scarest me with dreams, and terrifiest me through visions." The cure for our unrest is not a relapse into the womb of the unconscious but a rise into creative consciousness.

3. PAGANISM

In a world where intellectual, aesthetic and moral values are crumbling, the pleasures of sense are the only certainties. If the world of becoming, of change, of transiency is the only world, we must learn to be content with what we can see, hear, smell, touch and taste.[4] We are passing shadows, creatures of a moment and death is sure to lay us flat sometime or other. Pain, disease, unhappiness weigh down the scale heavily. Life is insignificant and death is without consequence. Failure is unimportant and success means nothing. Yet we are not born to be miserable, not born to waste the gift of life by complaining against the universe or murmuring against God. The mystics

[4] "Let us learn to gather sloes in their season, to shear sheep, to draw water from the spring with grateful happiness and no longer vex our hearts with impossible longings." Llewelyn Powys, *The Glory of Life* (1938), p. 47.

of the body exhort us to sink into sloth, "sit at home by the fire
and fatten a lazy body" as W. B. Yeats says in *The Celtic
Thought*, or spend our powers in restless activity, often meaningless, often we know not what.

The materialist philosophers of ancient India adopted an
attitude of unqualified hedonism:

> While life is yours, live joyously:
> None can escape Death's searching eye;
> When once this frame of ours they burn,
> How shall it e'er again return? [5]

This whole attitude of paganism is based on a fundamental
suspicion of life. Man hesitates between the call of the body
and the call of the spirit. The call of the body seems clear,
simple and natural and if man listens to it he ceases to grow
and slides back into slavery from which he is trying to liberate
himself slowly. By obeying his instincts, he lapses from the line
of evolution. When life is lacking in deep wells of quietness,
we make up for it by plunging into sensations. By these dis-
tractions we deaden our attention to the aching void in us.
The strain of adapting oneself to a world in confusion may be
great, but to eat, sleep, go about and rest with the belief that
nothing matters is a mental impossibility. Refined paganism is
not an answer to the problem of living.

4. HUMANISM

When the human mind finds that the props on which it has
leaned for long are rotten and rickety, when the traditional
creeds are suspected to be baseless, when life seems to lose its
meaning and gets shrivelled into a span, when a mood of

---

[5] yāvaj jīvet sukham jīvet, ṛṇam kṛtvā ghṛtam pibet
bhasmībhūtasya dehasya punar-āgamanam kutaḥ.

fearful insecurity and loneliness of spirit overtakes us, we feel that the only way to live sanely is by holding fast to those essential things which are certain still, the simplicity of truth and the majesty of the moral law. It is an awful hour and only those who have passed through it can say how awful, when death seems to be the end of all, the living universe becomes a dead expanse, and the sky above is black with the void from which the divine has departed.

Humanism is defined in the *Oxford Dictionary* as "any system of thought or action which is concerned with merely human interests (as distinguished from divine) or with those of the human race in general." For humanism man is the highest type of individual in existence and the service of man is the highest religion. It believes in the good life, in moderation, harmony, balance, while religion insists on another standard. Humanism assumes that man is by nature good and that evil rests in society, in the conditions which surround man, and if these are removed, man's goodness will emerge and progress will be achieved. Religion, on the other hand, believes in the radical insufficiency of human nature. The religious individual is tormented by the grim fact of sin and the dire necessity to escape from it.

Humanist revivals occur when religions disintegrate and fail to attract men's attention. It was so in ancient Greece. Protagoras' work on *Truth* has a striking saying, which finds an echo today: "Concerning the gods, I have not been able to *ascertain* whether they exist or not; the obscurity of the subject and the brevity of human life have hindered me from finding out." Confucius adopted a strictly rational view of knowledge. "To say that you know a thing when you know it and to say that you do not know when you do not know it, that is knowl-

edge." When questioned about death and the proper duties to
the gods, Confucius answered: "We know not about life, how
can we know death? And we have not learned how to serve
men, how can we serve gods?" [6] The popularity of the Stoic
creed in the Hellenistic period is, to no small extent, due to
the feeling that, at a time when men felt themselves to be
haunted by doubt and uncertainty, Stoicism asserted the existence of a few certainties in human experience.

When the Graeco-Roman world took over Christianity it
was a change from the enjoyment of human life in the gym-
nasium and in the theatre to a state of abnegation and austerity
which barely provided for the minimum necessities of life. The
free Greek spirit, critical and rebellious, with its insistence on
form, social and political freedom, rationalism was never completely reconciled with the Christian virtues of voluntary poverty and humility. There was a perpetual tension between the
two, expressing itself in the development of the heresies and
the disputations of the schools. In Europe, the religious state
of mind prevailed as an ideal from the third century A.D. until
the fifteenth. Humanists regretted this domination by religious
superstition and dismissed the view of life as a vale of tears
and since then humanist philosophy has increased in influence. [7]

[6] Hu Shih, *The Chinese Renaissance* (1934), p. 81.

[7] Cf. Sir James Frazer: "The saint and the recluse, disdainful of earth
and wrapt in ecstatic contemplation of Heaven, became in popular
opinion the highest ideal of humanity. The earthly city became poor and
contemptible to many whose eyes beheld the City of God coming in the
clouds of Heaven. . . . This obsession lasted for a thousand years. The
revival of Roman Law, of the Aristotelian philosophy, of Ancient Art
and Literature, at the close of the Middle Ages marked the return of
Europe to native ideals of life and conduct, to saner, manlier views of
the world. The long halt of civilization was over. The tide of Oriental
invasion had turned at last. It is ebbing still." *The Golden Bough* (1914),
pp. 299–301. Stephen McKenna, the brilliant translator of Plotinus'

The leaders of the eighteenth-century enlightenment cultivated an optimistic attitude to life with an active ethics of enthusiastic devotion to human welfare. Humanism became the secular religion and its practical results were seen in the Declaration of the Rights of Man and the French Revolution. Many intellectuals of our generation adopt humanism as a comforting and reasonable attitude.[8]

In the last chapter of *Principia Ethica,* Professor G. E. Moore sums up his own views. In Section II, 3, he writes:

> By far the most valuable things we know or can imagine are certain states of consciousness, which may roughly be described as the pleasures of human intercourse and the enjoyment of beautiful objects. This simple truth may, indeed,

Enneads, said: "That Christianity instead of Platonism became the religion of the later ages is the eternal proof of the imbecility of man." Dodds, *Journal and Letters of Stephen McKenna* (1936), p. 21.

[8] Look at the following extract from Galsworthy's *Flowering Wilderness,* Chap. VI:

"What proportion of people in these days do you think really have religion, Uncle?"

"In northern countries? Very difficult to say. In this country ten to fifteen percent of the adults, perhaps. In France and Southern countries, where there is a peasantry more at least on the surface . . ."

"Are you a Christian, Uncle Lawrence?"

"No, my dear, if anything a Confucian, and Confucius, as you know, was simply an ethical philosopher. Most of our caste in this country, if they only knew it, are Confucian rather than Christian. Belief in ancestors and tradition, respect for parents, honesty, kind treatment of animals and dependents, absence of self-obtrusion and stoicism in face of pain and death. What more . . . does one want except the love of beauty?" Cf. E. M. Forster's *A Passage to India* (1924), p. 109. Fielding, the central figure of the novel, who represents liberal culture—humanity, disinterestedness, tolerance, free intelligence, unmixed with any dogma or religious tradition, when asked, "Is it correct that most are atheists in England now?" replies: "The educated thoughtful people, I should say so, though they don't like the name. The truth is that the West doesn't bother much over belief and disbelief in these days. Fifty years ago, or even when you and I were young, much more fuss was made."

THE NEED FOR BELIEF

be said to be universally recognised. What has *not* been recognised is that it is the ultimate and fundamental truth of Moral Philosophy. That it is only for the sake of these things—in order that as much of them as possible may at some time exist—that any one can be justified in performing any public or private duty; that they are the *raison d'être* of virtue, that it is they—these complex wholes themselves, and not any constituent or characteristic of them—that form the rational ultimate end of human action.

The book was published in 1903. For the young intellectuals of that period to whom dogmatic religion was unacceptable, Moore provided a way out. His states of consciousness are spiritual states, essentially religious. Moore insisted on the intrinsic value of human relations and exhorted his disciples to multiply instances of his two most valuable things, friendship and beauty, and not the pursuit of personal power and success.

There are few human beings who are without a sense of curiosity or wonder and even of awe when they look at this vast universe. Man is eager to know the nature of the universe, its source and destiny. Our belief in human values requires us to be integrated with our view of the universe.

Again, in defining the nature of man, we cannot exclude a reference to the spirit in him, what Aristotle describes as "that which is better than reason, being the source of reason." [9] Humanism overlooks the immortal longings, the intimations of sanctity, the hunger and thirst for holiness, the readiness to suffer persecution and martyrdom.

[9] *Eudemian Ethics.* Cf. A. N. Whitehead: "Our minds are finite, and yet even in these circumstances of finitude, we are surrounded by possibilities that are infinite, and the purpose of human life is to grasp as much as we can of that infinitude." *Dialogues of Alfred North Whitehead* by Lucien Price (1954).

E

There is a Platonism native to our minds, a preference for eternal values. In Canto IV of the *Inferno,* Dante gives us a picture of Limbo, which is the home of Vergil and Homer, the great poets of antiquity, of Aristotle and great philosophers, of Hector, Aeneas, Caesar and other heroes. The highest happiness that man as man can hope for, by his philosophic thought, artistic creation, moral and political effort is life without suffering but not life without sighing.[10] These noble thinkers, artists and heroes did "nothing wrong," but their merits were for them neither grace on earth nor glory in the world to come. So is it that "without hope they live in desire." This is all the happiness, according to Dante, that humanism

[10] *Inferno,* IV, 26. There is a famous passage in the Autobiography of *John Stuart Mill:* "From the winter of 1821, when I first read Bentham, and especially from the commencement of the *Westminster Review,* I had what might truly be called an object in life; to be a reformer of the world. My conception of my own happiness was entirely identified with this object. The personal sympathies I wished for were those of fellow-labourers, in this enterprise. I endeavoured to pick up as many flowers as I could by the way; but as a serious and permanent personal satisfaction to rest upon, my whole reliance was placed on this; and I was accustomed to felicitate myself on the certainty of a happy life which I enjoyed, through placing my happiness in something durable and distant, in which some progress might be always making, while it could never be exhausted by complete attainment. . . . But the time came when I awakened from this as from a dream. It was in the autumn of 1826. I was in a dull state of nerves, such as everybody is occasionally liable to. . . . In this frame of mind it occurred to me to put the question directly to myself: 'Suppose that all your objects in life were realised; that all the changes in institutions and opinions which you are looking forward to, could be completely effected at this very instant; would this be a great joy and happiness to you?' And an impressive self-consciousness distinctly answered, 'No.' At this my heart sank within me; the whole foundation on which my life was constructed fell down. All my happiness was to have been found in the continued pursuit of this end. The end has ceased to charm and how could there ever again be any interest in the means? I seem to have nothing left to live for." J. S. Mill felt that he should give "its proper place, among the prime necessities of human well-being, to the internal culture of the individual."

offers. Aristotle, the master of those that know, "lives there," but that place is not paradise. Dante is not quite fair to Aristotle, who holds that the purest and least selfish satisfaction known to man is seeking knowledge for its own sake. Inexhaustible is the happiness of pure knowing. It is to share the activity of God himself, his eternal life of pure contemplation.[11]

Humanism is a legitimate protest against those forms of religion which separate the secular and the sacred, divide time and eternity and break up the unity of soul and flesh. Religion is all or nothing. Every religion should have sufficient respect for the dignity of man and the rights of human personality. We cannot preserve them, if we repudiate religion. As the Indian visitor is reported to have said to Socrates, if we do not know about God we cannot know about man.[12] Religion is the perfection of the truly human. Humanism today is in search of a soul.

5. NATIONALISM

The tribal character of religion can be traced to early times when the function of religion was said to be the training of its adherents to a patriotic docility. Yahveh, as the God of Israel, represented the national consciousness, the hopes and aspirations of Israel. The Jews belonged to one great family, one tribe. "O Jerusalem, if I forget thee, let my right hand forget its cunning: if I do not remember thee, let my tongue cleave to the roof of my mouth, if I prefer not Jerusalem above my chief joy." [13] Every Greek village had its special tree or spring

[11] *Nichomachean Ethics,* X, 7–8.
[12] "They that deny a God deny Man's nobility, for certainly Man is kin to the Beast by his Body, and if he is not kin to God by his Spirit he is a base ignoble creature." Bacon.
[13] Psalm 137:5–6.

or shrine devoted to the worship of some god or hero who specially protected its people. In Japan religion is used for the consolidation of the state. Muhammad is the founder of a faith and a nation. In weak and subject countries, nationalism has become a religion. By appealing to the elemental sense of self-respect, it inspires a confused and struggling people to positive action. It gives them self-confidence, a sense of unity and a belief in the mission of their country.

Even those who profess to be religious exalt the nation-state. In almost all countries, the religion taught in educational institutions is some local variant of Shintoism, a saluting of flags and a singing of national anthems. Someone said: "England has a religion; her religion is England."

Nationalism is a political religion which stirs the hearts and wills of men and rouses them to service and self-sacrifice in a way that no purely religious movements have done in recent times. It speaks with the accents of authority and appeals to our emotions. Nations claim to be the highest manifestation of divine purpose in the world.[14] The German Christians affirmed: "Through Hitler, Christ has become mighty amongst us. Therefore National Socialism is positive Christianity in action." [15]

Religion must be catholic, universal, applicable to all classes and conditions of men. Nationalism militates against this spirit. No religion can claim to follow the right way unless it ceases to be a function of a group, class or nation. The worship of a

[14] Cf. Kipling's well-known lines from "The Recessional":
> God of our fathers, known of old—
> Lord of our far-flung battle-line—
> Beneath whose awful hand we hold
> Dominion over palm and pine.

[15] Quoted in A. Firey, *Cross and Swastika* (1938), p. 12.

group, even though it may be the nation, reduces God to an attribute of nationality. When a nation thinks itself divine and believes that it alone is fit and destined to raise up and save all the rest by its truth, love of power and dominion springs up.

6. COMMUNISM

The vast historical phenomenon which, in one generation, has overthrown old orders, revolutionised widely disparate societies, effected the greatest redistribution of political, economic and military power the world has ever known, which has succeeded over nearly half the world and is felt to be a challenge to the rest, requires study and understanding. We should try to know its intellectual content, its ethical programme, its social passion. There are many people in the world who are eager to resist communism but not many are aware of what it is they are up against. We cannot rebut an idea, refute a claim, or offer a counter-attraction to an appeal unless we first know what the idea, the claim and the appeal are. If the spy stories, the midnight arrests, the heresy persecutions, the recantations by former Communists who endured the change from faith to disillusion, the military interventions, the liquidations of large sections of the community are all that we have to urge, we do not get to the root of the matter.

Marxists believe that they have developed a scientific view of the nature of man. As a social being, his nature is determined by the way in which the necessaries of life are produced. His consciousness is a function of his social situation. His mentality is the superstructure built on the foundation of the economic relations by which the necessaries of life are supplied. Philosophies are ideologies which have developed in order to justify the particular interests that dominate in a given situa-

tion. Classes change in accordance with changes in the means
of production. With the two classes of workers and capitalists
today, the state is a means of class domination by which one
class keeps the other in a condition of subordination. Religion
is the opium by which the members of the subordinate class
are doped and kept in a condition of contented dependence.
Class conflict is inevitable in the transient phase in the development of the means of production. When this phase is got over,
a classless society will arise, where there will be no exploitation
and there will be no need for the state also. In that society the
needs of all will be supplied and there will be perfect justice
and full scope for freedom. During the present phase of history we are advancing towards this goal. The members of the
Communist Party, who actively will the attainment of the goal,
are the spearhead of the march towards the future.

Communism condemns religion because it assumes that it is
a type of transcendental idealism, whose heaven is outside the
historical process. If religion takes any interest in worldly affairs, it does so only to protect the privileges of the rich and
the powerful. The Communist ideal is this-worldly and the
rewards it promises are to be enjoyed here on earth. It does
not preach patience and resignation; it is a call to effort and
endeavour, to struggle and sacrifice to make a new society.
However fantastic and outrageous many of its hopes and doctrines may be, communism is groping towards a new ideal
based on the principle, "sell all that thou hast and give to the
poor"—a principle we all admire but do not care to practice.
Its appeal is wide. The intellectuals who are tired of a way of
life which seems intolerably tame because it makes no demands
are attracted to it. Making money all the time is not a very
exciting occupation. The workers are persuaded that they can

escape from their dull and drab, poor and limited lives. Communism seems to offer a way of escape from a world without faith, without the understanding of the malaise of the age and without the will to overcome it. It gives all those who are suffering from fear and ambition, from cynicism and despair a cause which seems capable of evoking life from death.

The urge to self-transcendence cannot be suppressed. As traditional religions are deficient, other ways are devised, art and music, dance and demagogy. Communism is the most powerful of these ways of escape. Young men and women are rediscovering that there is a joy, an exhilaration in devotion to a cause beside which a life of ease, pleasure and self-indulgence looks stale and tawdry. By joining a group and marching in step to the singing of tunes, we escape from the torments of self and are relieved of personal responsibilities.

Communism has all the characteristics of a religion [16] though it is entirely secular and humanist. It teaches as absolutely true a clear-cut philosophy of man and nature. If we make a certain kind of political and economic revolution, general well-being will follow. It asserts an infallibility and imposes an orthodoxy. It is not a mere reasoned interpretation of the universe, for its appeal for justice has all the force of a religion. It is moved by a conviction that is as profound as religious faith. It is persuaded that no sacrifices are too great for the attainment of its ideal.

Every true religion has a note of revolutionary challenge. This note has disappeared in established religions, which have become purely formal. Communism has captured this note.

---

[16] John Middleton Murry goes to the extent of saying that "communism is the one living religion in the Western world today." *The Necessity of Communism* (1932), p. 111.

Stalin's funeral utterance over Lenin is well-known; "We vow to you, Comrade Lenin, that we will not spare our lives to strengthen and extend the union of the toilers of the whole world."

The reliance of the Communists on Marx, Engels, Lenin and Stalin reminds one of the dependence of religious people on scriptural texts. As a matter of fact, there is hardly any phase in the history of communism that has not its parallel in the history of Christianity. We have catacombs, sacred books, dogmas, tedious exegeses, schismatics, martyrs, heretics, purges, saints, sinners and paradise beyond the present vale of tears. Its methods and discipline remind one forcibly of certain religious orders. It believes with religion that the world is on the brink of an apocalyptic cataclysm, an impending doom, that history is intolerably slow, that truth and justice must be established on earth without delay, doubt or compromise. The late Nicholas Berdyaev, a religious philosopher with an inside knowledge of Russian communism, suggests that the attitude of communism to religion is so hostile because "it wants to be a religion itself." [17] "It is built," he says, "after the pattern of the Catholic and Orthodox theocracies, but the pattern is reversed." [18] Communism is belief without God; it is the religion of atheism.

When we condemn communism as an evil disease which is spreading widely and menacing the non-Communist world from without and undermining it from within, threatening to destroy the great values of Western civilisation, we do not seem to realise that it professes to be the consistent development of the values of liberalism which are an integral part of Western

[17] *The Origin of Russian Communism* (1937), p. 191.
[18] *Ecumenical Review*, No. 1 (1948), p. 23.

civilisation. Communism is the logical sequel to the liberal tradition of eighteenth-century Europe of Locke, Montesquieu
and Rousseau, who pleaded for a reorganisation of society
which would enable every man to live his own life in his own
way provided he respected the rights of others to do likewise.
From the concepts of justice and equality are derived the social
protests, "that rocked Western society, transformed it and still
shake its structure." The Communist ideal, as expressed in the
last paragraph of the second section of the *Communist Manifesto,* "an association in which the free development of each is
the condition of the free development of all," is accepted by
all liberal thinkers of East and West.[19]

The demand to change society so that men's lives may be
made rich, free and happy is a logical corollary of the religious
principle that we are all the children of God. Communism developed because religious people betrayed their responsibility.
The famous last thesis on Feuerbach maintains that "the philosophers have only interpreted the world differently, the point
is, however, to change it." What communism attempts to do
is to change the world and not merely be content with the
interpretations given by Christian religion and secular humanism. Communism may well be called a Christian heresy,
a heresy because it is opposed to Christian orthodoxy but not
necessarily to Christian truth and Christian principles. An
equitable social order remained with religions a mere intention, while there is a serious attempt to accomplish it in communism. No one can read Marx's *Kapital* without becoming

---

[19] Lord Acton observes in an unpublished diary: "We may see an error
in Marx. But where does it come from? A[dam] Smith, Malthus, Ricardo,
N[ew] T[estament], Plato, Fathers, Canon Law, [Sir Thomas] More,
Divines." Cambridge University Library Additional Manuscripts 5638,
quoted in *Times Literary Supplement,* May 28, 1954, p. 345.

aware of his burning indignation against social wrong and earnest concern for raising the conditions of the poor and the oppressed.[20] Communism is a judgment on the defects of religious practice. Jacques Maritain observes: "Communism originates chiefly through the fault of a Christian world unfaithful to its own principles, in a profound sense of *resentment,* not only against the Christian world but—and here lies the tragedy—against Christianity itself which transcends the Christian world." [21]

The 1948 Lambeth Conference of Bishops called upon Christian people to recognise that in communism there are "elements which are a true judgment on the existing social and economic order." [22] Russia looked upon the 1917 revolution as the dawn of personal liberty, opportunity for the intelligent poor and freedom for national minorities.

An idea common to all the radical thinkers of the nineteenth century is that political power is oppressive and is essentially

[20] Berdyaev writes: "The Russian people in full accordance with their particular mentality offered themselves as a burnt offering on the altar of an experiment unknown to previous history; they have demonstrated the extremest consequences of certain ideas. They are an apocalyptic people and they could not stop short at a compromise, at some 'humanitarian state.' They had to make real either brotherhood in Christ or comradeship in Anti-Christ. If the one does not reign, then the other will. The people of Russia have put this choice before the whole world with awe-inspiring force." *The End of Our Time* (1933).

[21] *True Humanism,* Eng. translation (1938), p. 33. Professor John Macmurray maintains that in practice communism is more truly Christian than Christianity itself. He says: "If we put *profession* on one side, and consider only the *attitude of mind* which is expressed in the communist way of life, we begin to wonder whether there is not something peculiarly religious about it, which is missing in the attitude which is generally characteristic of professedly Christian communities. . . . I cannot help feeling that Communism . . . has recovered that essential core of a real belief in God, which organised Christianity has in our day largely lost." *Creative Society* (1935), pp. 22 ff.

[22] Resolutions 25 and 26.

evil. For Marx, it is the instrument of the idle and the privileged, who use it for exploiting the workers. But it is a necessary evil during the time of the political struggle. It will disappear only after the workers have captured it and used it to change the structure of society but not till then.[23] The inclination for anarchy and the need for security require to be reconciled. When knowledge grows, industry is perfected and men have the material and spiritual resources enabling them to live as members of free societies, the need for violence and exploitation terminates. The withering of the state is intended to foster the freedom of the human spirit. The ideal society of Marx is a society of equals, where none could use force to impose his will on others. He criticised bourgeois democracy because in such a society the rights of man were the privilege of a small minority. Only in a classless society will every man be free to make the best use of his life according to his own notions of what is good. Such a

[23] Engels writes: "As soon as there is no longer any class of society to be held in subjection . . . there is nothing more to be repressed, which would make a special repressive force, a state necessary. The first act whereby the state really comes forward as the representative of society as a whole—the taking possession of the means of production in the name of society—is also its last independent act as a state. . . . The government of persons is replaced by the administration of things and the direction of the processes of production. The state is not abolished, it withers away." *Anti-Dubring* III, 2. Lenin, following Marx, says, "Only in Communist society, when the resistance of the capitalists has been completely broken, when the capitalists have disappeared, when there are no classes . . . only then will really complete democracy, democracy without any exceptions be possible and be realised. And only then will democracy itself begin to *wither away* owing to the simple fact, that freed from capitalist slavery . . . people will gradually become accustomed to observing the elementary rules of social life that have been known for centuries and repeated for thousands of years in all copy book maxims; they will become accustomed to observing them without force, without compulsion, without subordination, without the special apparatus for compulsion which is called the state." Christopher Hill, *Lenin and the Russian Revolution* (1947), p. 110.

society is possible if the material resources of the community are controlled for the common good by those responsible to the community.

We must distinguish between the social philosophy of communism and the technique of government which Communist countries adopt to implement the theory. For no political doctrine remains unchanged, when it inspires political practice.

It is unfortunate that Marx felt that the new society could not be established without a long, bitter and uncompromising struggle. According to the *Communist Manifesto* of 1848, "Communists disdain to conceal the fact that their ends can be attained only by the forcible overthrow of all existing social conditions." Marx, therefore, advocated the use of coercion and violence. He characterised those who hoped to reach the same ideal by mild and less painful processes Utopians and called himself scientific. He was a revolutionary asking for bold and quick action, while the socialists were reformist. What distinguishes "scientists" from Utopians is their revolutionary zeal. But we can achieve a classless society without a violent revolution. The character of the revolution is determined by the men who take charge of it. Lord Acton, who was no radical, referred to revolution as "the modern method of progress." Its function is to "shake off the past" and "rescue the world from the reign of the dead." We can have bloodless revolutions. The totalitarian character of modern communism is illiberal, unrighteous and, one may even say, un-Marxist.

Violence becomes necessary only if the privileged classes give up the rule of law and resort to violence.[24] Bourgeois democ-

---

[24] Engels writes: "We, the 'revolutionaries,' the 'rebels,' we are thriving far better on legal than on illegal methods of revolt. The parties of order . . . are perishing under the legal conditions created by themselves. They cry in despair with Odilon Barrot, *la légalité nous tue,*

racies in Western Europe are giving greater opportunities for
workers than they had ever enjoyed in other parts of the
world. Today in countries which have adopted parliamentary
democracy, workers are much better off than elsewhere. They
are better housed, fed, clothed and educated than they had
ever been. No society can remain free and secure unless the just
claims of all its sections are conceded. Bourgeois democracies,
when Marx and Engels were young, were much less proletarian
than they are today.

Communists seem to be as bad as the worst religious dog-
matists quoting their scriptures all the time. If they give up
their closed minds, they will realise that there is no scientific
evidence for their beliefs that the cultural and economic pattern of societies is uniquely determined by the character of the
forces of production, or that the main causes of war are economic or that socialism cannot develop in a variety of ways
which need not all be of a totalitarian type. We cannot defend
a rigid orthodoxy in a changing world. We must be scientific,
realistic, open-minded and creative in our outlook and approach. We must take into account the progressive trends in
parliamentary democracies which are more favourable to the
workers than to the privileged classes. It is to go against all
facts to assert that the working class will not secure their rights
without a fight and force is the only midwife which will give
birth to a new society. The Communists, who advocate revolutionary socialism, forget that peaceful revolutions are also possible and it is not wise to exploit the fears, hopes and hatreds
of the ordinary people in the interests of a dogma.

While communism states clearly the problem of social jus-

legality is the death of us; while we, under this legality, get firm muscles
and rosy cheeks, and look like living for ever." Quoted in John Plam-
enatz's *German Marxism and Russian Communism* (1954), p. 166.

tice, it has made a fatal blunder in disregarding the rights of the individual. While all social systems must accept the challenge of the necessity of world-wide social change, they should all treat the individual with justice and charity. In totalitarian systems the rights of the individual are suppressed.

Simply because we have a classless society, it does not follow that all people are homogeneous and their interests can be represented by one party. The one-party system is devised to defend the new types of inequalities which are springing up and perpetuating themselves. Russia has not developed the solidarity, the common brotherhood between all classes of society. The social barriers are still there. As in the Tsarist times, we have a privileged class at the top and at the base a mass of workers and peasants who are ignorant of the meaning of freedom and justice and without the means to improve their lot. The monolithic state where all forms of power, economic, political and even religious, are fused at the summit of the social pyramid, where a few men know all, do all and decide all, does not fulfil the humanist ideal which Marx had in view. If we are led to believe that life is a meaningless accident, that we are homeless in the vast cold black spaces, that our humanity is without any sense or dignity, then we do not mind if our essential rights are taken away from us.

Welfare states may be proletarian and Communist states may be bourgeois. The old distinctions seem to be losing their point. Parliamentary democracies satisfy the two principles laid down by Kant: freedom is obedience to the law we prescribe for ourselves and it is morally wrong for any man to treat another merely as a means to his own ends. In a monolithic state, these principles are not protected. If communism is to be true to the principles of freedom and humanism which it proclaims, a change in the system of government is called for. When we do not permit obvious and open forms of opposition, secret movements spring up. The insecurity to the individual is most harassing. A person may be a minister today and a prisoner tomorrow. He is honoured by one chief and disgraced by another. As standards rise and as people become educated and capable of thinking for themselves, they will become critical of the monolithic state and will be unable to defend it.

There is a sense of anticipatory uneasiness in Soviet Russia. The present rulers seem to be aware of it, and are attempting, subject to the limitations of what they have inherited, an improvement in the protection of the individual's rights and impartial justice.

The view of the individual adopted by the Communists reduces him to a slave or an automaton. According to Hegel, the individual's conscious will is insignificant beside his real will, which is moulded by his national culture. This national culture is identified with the will of the state and the actions of the state are governed by the laws of the dialectic of history. Marx inverts this view and suggests an alternative explanation. He says: "It is not the consciousness of men that determines their existence, but rather, it is their social existence that determines their consciousness."

In his anxiety for social reform, Marx traces all evil and imperfections to bad external conditions. Man's moral condition in the past was bad because the social order was bad. It was a class structure in which a great mass of mankind existed only because they sold their labour to the owners of the means of production, who exploited the need of the workers, giving to each worker only so much of the proceeds as was necessary to keep him alive and reasonably fit, appropriating the rest for their own use. If we replace this system by communism we will help both the rich and the poor. The rich will give up their ostentation, arrogance, selfishness and snobbery and the poor will be rid of their ignorance, servility and degradation.

It is true that man becomes rational and moral in society but it does not follow that social interests are more important than personal relationships. A plant cannot live without earth, air and water, but it is something different from them all. We are not wholly social beings always dressed for a part. What is happening in man's soul, heart and mind, what springs up there or what withers away is important for a man's life. We must respect the soul's hidden depths from which arise all great art, science and literature. For Marx, the individual is more important than society, and that society is best organised where every member is able to lead a full and free life. If we ignore this fundamental objective, what is set before us as a worthy object of our devotion is only an idol of collective human power.

There are many social evils which are the products of circumstances—ugliness, dirt, disease and malnutrition—but all evil is not of economic origin. The passions of the human heart, the callous indifference to human suffering, the lust for domination, these strands of evil are inextricably woven into our make-up. The doctrine of original sin is not the discovery of the theologian. The innate obstinacy of human nature cannot be overcome by changes in the environment. The Marxist hope is wholly materialist and devoid of any sense of mystery. Man is intended not only to understand and construct but also to wonder and admire. Sciences give us power, not vision, strength, not sanction. Man is not body and mind; he is also spirit.

It is in the name of the individual that Marx criticised bourgeois society. It is therefore strange to hear his followers speak of the rights of the individual as a hypocritical expression of the capitalist society's preoccupation with the safeguarding of its privileges. All progress is due to individual effort. Decisive inventions originate with individuals. If they do not have freedom, progress will be arrested.

When we accuse the Communists that their governments are condemning millions to hard labour, they either deny the charge, or account for it by saying that it is one of the harsh necessities of a period of transition. We cannot make omelettes without breaking eggs. They show a total deficiency of imagination if they believe that people will put up with conditions where there is no respect for law and truth.

One of the claims of communism is that it is international. It teaches that the working classes of different nations have more interests in common than the different classes in the same nation. We are not aiming at a vague cosmopolitanism. Any international society is to be built on the basis of nations. The workers in the last two wars had not generally betrayed their countries. When they did not share in the people's mood and accepted dictation from outside, they were convicted of treachery. The easy victory of the Nazis over the German Communists is not to be accounted for only by their mere unscrupulous methods. It is also due to the fact that the German Communists were shown up as being controlled from abroad.

The dispute between Trotsky and Stalin centred round the international character of communism. Before there could be real socialism in Russia, Trotsky felt that there should be a

F

proletarian revolution in some at least of the more advanced
neighbouring countries. As against this view, Stalin maintained
that one country could become Socialist even though other
neighbouring countries may be of the bourgeois type; only the
Socialist country cannot be secure in a predominantly capitalist world.

If the Russians suffered meekly the burdens imposed on
them, it was because they were persuaded that if Russia did
not grow strong quickly, she would be exposed to attack from
the foreigners. The patriotic sentiments of the people were
utilised for the building up of a Socialist state. Again, there are
no ideological differences between Soviet Russia and Yugoslavia. Yugoslavia respects its own independence and will not
allow itself to be treated as a colony of a foreign state. The
Communist states wish to be treated as equals and not sub-
ordinates. Communism in China is popular because it is not
felt to be alien. Nationalism is yet a powerful sentiment.[25]
However powerful and fertile ideas from abroad may be they
can strike root and become acclimatised only if they meet the
country's own needs. We cannot develop societies to order on
the lines of programmes borrowed from others.

If we are interested in halting the spread of communism, we
must grapple with the great social and political problems of
the age. Countries which have developed a complex social
structure and an advanced form of economic organisation, do

[25] The Archbishop of Canterbury said after Russia's entry into the
Second World War: "It is significant that on the outbreak of war thousands flocked to churches for prayer in Moscow and elsewhere," and he
added, "It may well be that Russia's defence of its own land and the new
unity which this will bring may lead to a new tolerance of religion by the
Soviet Government, a new resurgence of the interests of religion, always
deep seated in the hearts of the Russian people."

not, as a rule, take kindly to communism. Those who suffer from mass misery will follow any reform movement that offers them the hope of better things. If there is an already established liberal tradition they will develop it on the lines of social democracy. They will replace reformist capitalism by democratic socialism as in England. If there is no liberal tradition as in Soviet Russia, authoritarian movements succeed.

Religion requires us to appeal to the higher instincts of man, reason, co-operation, love, and not to fear, greed and hatred. Yet revolutionary movements derive their dynamic thrust from the passion of hate and not love. This hate is directed against some group of human beings, chosen as scapegoats, the Jews, the Christians, the Capitalists or the Communists. While the Communists and the non-Communists have similar conceptions of the ultimate ends of social life, and believe in the interdependence of means and ends, they are not agreed about the mutual relations of means and ends. Both no doubt count the cost in terms of human happiness.

Religion assumes that human nature, however depraved, will always respond to the power of goodness. The story of Jesus relates the rejection of absolute goodness by the world. Jesus may have refused to lead his disciples to the establishment of an earthly kingdom by military force but Christian states which are called upon to maintain a just order in human affairs are not precluded from the use of physical force. The saints who are concerned with the winning and healing of souls do not use coercive methods, since the latter are unfitted by their very nature for the attainment of spiritual ends. In an imperfect world it is not always possible to pursue a line of action which is ideally perfect. Both the Communists and the non-Communist states agree that physical force should not be used for purposes of aggression and even in repelling aggression not more force should be used than is absolutely necessary.

Ruthlessness as a major temptation is nothing new; only the magnitude and the dangers entailed are novel and unique. Logically speaking, the difference between shooting a man in cold blood as part of a campaign of terror and the destruction of a city for strategic purposes is one of degree, not kind. When we admit that it is permissible for us to use force in the interests of expediency, there is a confusion between means and ends. The difference between the Communist and the non-Communist states, on this matter, is only a matter of degree and not of principle or intention.

Those who live on earth by the light of God should affirm in these solemn moments that the slightest touch of expediency poisons the pure substance of the spirit. A single ray of darkness is enough to blot out a world of light. In our crusading zeal we are unaware of the demoralising effects of violence on both those who employ it and those who suffer from it. Totalitarian systems moved to desperation by the inertia of the masses and the indifference of the classes, forget the final ends man sets to himself and turn the means into ends. Power is sought for its own sake. The universal morality is relegated to a distant future and an interim ethics based on the class struggle occupies the central place. The universal morality of the classless millennium is used to condemn the acts of our opponents while the interim ethics justifies the actions of the revolutionaries. The non-totalitarian systems in their zeal are also tempted to adopt the interim ethics.

Peoples of the world are very much like one another. We should not believe in the simplicities of right and wrong. The world is often divided into areas of black and white. There are no shades in between and these areas have changed pretty violently in the last decade or two. Any area which is regarded as black is represented as wholly evil and we, assumed to be virtuous, should have nothing to do with something which is wholly evil.

This is, however, the doctrine of Manichaeism, which believes in two principles controlling the universe, the Power of God and the Power of Evil equally active, independent and indispensable. The truth is that the duality is within each one's nature. The baser elements in us are the habitation of the Devil. Our torturing obsessions, our fanaticisms for or against communism are the temptations of the Evil One. Our love of humanity, our anxiety for peace and co-operative living, are the expressions of the Divine in us. God and the Devil are fighting in each one of us. The battlefield is the heart of man. "If we say that we have no sin, we deceive ourselves, and the truth is not in us." [26] In no human institution or individual do we encounter sheer, unadulterated evil, active, deliberate, deadly. We come across folly, heedlessness, vanity, craft, ambition, pride, meanness, stupidity. We and our "enemies" are all victims of these faults.

The insufficiency of communism may be brought out by a reference to the three temptations of Jesus. Most of the people in the world hunger for bread, for material security. If Jesus had been the leader of an economic revolution, he would have been accepted by the people, but man does not live by bread alone. If he performed miracles, he would have won the allegiance of the masses. He would not attract the crowds by a display of his miraculous powers. If he had consented to use violence and subdue the kingdom of this world and make of

[26] I John 1:8.

mankind one great community, he would have had a large following. He did not worship power or accept violence. He set the freedom of the human spirit above material comfort, religious submission or superstition and world dominion.

In a Communist society, it is the human spirit that does not get a chance. When we join the party, the group feeling gives the necessary exhilaration, the illusion of inward strength and worthwhileness. We get excited about the party even as we do about wars. It gives us a common cause, something outside for which we can live and die, the ecstasy of a new religious life, the chivalry of a new crusade. This peace is the result not of inward strength but of submission to the objective.

In communism there is little of the pursuit of truth, no passion for individual integrity, and spiritual perfection, no faith in the inwardness of human life. Any kind of totalitarianism, political or religious, contains within it the seeds of its own decline. It may, for a time, remove from men's minds the sense of fear, doubt and uncertainty, but it cannot produce lasting results. It provides security only so long as our minds are closed to other influences. However imperfect our minds and spirits may be, they cannot forever be persuaded to eschew the critical functioning of intelligence, which asks of every dogma, is it true? and of every priest and dictator, are they necessary? The assault on individual integrity will inevitably undermine the Communist faith.

However efficient we may be in our work, however comfortable we may be in our lives, on the Communist scheme we are empty within. The question is sometimes asked: Does the soul survive the death of the body? Whatever the answer may be, there is no doubt that often the soul is dead even when the body is alive.

The other principal defect of communism is that while religious people, whatever their practice may be, believe that love should be for all men, even our enemies, the Communists encourage hatred of the enemies, even the most ruthless action against them. Religions proclaim a universal morality. Each individual, irrespective of his class or nationality, bears the divine image. Spiritual love is universal in its significance. Unfortunately, even religions divided men into two groups, the Jew and the Gentile, the Christian and the heathen. They developed hostility and hatred towards infidels, schismatics. On the same principle, the Communists divide the world into two, those like themselves who are in the light and others who are in darkness. We cannot compromise with the enemy; we cannot deal with the devil. We must defeat him and stamp him out. This attitude is wrong and cruel. When Marx condemns capitalism, bourgeoisie, he adopts the universal standard of morality that capitalism dehumanizes men, turns them into things, mere instruments of economic progress. In condemning economic exploitation and demanding a Socialist structure of society, Marxism adopts a standard which is valid for everyone. If a Socialist society makes man a cog in the social machine, Marxism will have to condemn it, or the grounds for its condemnation of capitalism disappear. It is wrong for Marxists to think that the bourgeoisie is evil and the proletariat is good. They exalt class above man. It is our ambition to transform the whole society into a human community. What makes communism a parody of religion is its repudiation of the sanctity of human life with its dignity and conscience, intellectual and ethical, and its denunciation of the universal code of love.

Communists should realise that the works of Marx arose

from a special historical context and do not have a validity that transcends time. As the context has become profoundly modified, the system also requires drastic changes. When the two systems undergo radical changes, communism incorporating individual liberties and democracies fighting for justice in nations and among nations, the present conflict will fade away.

7. AUTHORITARIANISM

When faith is replaced by orthodoxy, the latter demands only obedience. Scepticism has no chance against the craving for authority. Attempts to reconcile critical scholarship with religious faith are dismissed as pernicious. We must have roots and we cannot have them unless we conform to tradition transmitted to us by a Holy Book or an established Church. In a period of social slackness, religious conservatism is extolled. The old has vanished, the new is nebulous. Nothing in human life holds good. Where can we discover peace of mind except in the Word of God, which will stand fast when all the host of heaven is dissolved and when the skies are rolled up like a scroll? When there is no hope on this side of the grave with its wars and rumours of wars, concentration camps and hydrogen bombs, we are inclined to place our trust in a Kingdom which is in heaven and on an authority that guarantees a safe transfer.

When we adopt an absolutist faith, we will not produce free spirits but only men and women of fanatical fervour. Reverence for authority which excludes free investigation turns religion itself into a superstition. The Mormons, for example, believe that Joseph Smith of Palmyra, New York, was visited by an angel who showed him a set of golden tablets pointing out that the inhabitants of America before Columbus were descended from the Jews. Not only this but he read the tablets through a pair of golden spectacles which turned their refined Hebrew writing into English. They have a single revelation which contains complete answers to all life's problems, a party and a leader.

When we repudiate reason and demand faith, we play into the hands of dictators who profess to supply us with definite creeds for belief and codes for conduct. In a lecture which Karl Barth gave at Oxford in 1938, he said: "The Christian Church in Germany was asked to recognise that what occurred in 1933 was a divine revelation which she had in future to take as seriously as what she had hitherto regarded and announced as the revelation of God in Jesus Christ." As a totalitarian faith is neither liberal nor democratic, it becomes easily an ally of political totalitarianism.[27] These authoritarian creeds overlook the value of individual freedom, of personal integrity.

The *Bhagavadgītā* opens with Arjuna's refusal to conform to the social code of a warrior. He insists that his conduct should be determined by his own self and not imposed on him by society. He preferred alienation from society, if necessary, to alienation from himself. The teacher explains the metaphysical background of the universe and leaves Arjuna to decide for himself.[28] Arjuna should not act from mere habit or obedience to authority. He must guard his integrity and see to it that his

---

[27] Archbishop William Temple wrote in 1943: "I think that an authoritarian organisation of religion is always bound to find itself lined up on the whole with authoritarian politics." See F. A. Iremonger, *Life of William Temple* (1948), p. 419. Karl Barth's recent statement on anti-Semitism is an indication of this warning. "Anti-semitism is right. . . . Israel is an evil people." *The Knowledge of God* (1937), p. 60. It was a Christian minister in the U.S.A. who revived the Ku Klux Klan in 1915 with the slogan, "Protestant Christianity and White Supremacy." See the article on *Ku Klux Klan* in *Encyclopaedia Britannica* (1946), Vol. XIII.

[28] XVIII.63.

decisions are his own. The passion for personal integrity is stronger in free spirits than love of ease and comfort.

The modern classic on the subject is Dostoevsky's "The Legend of the Grand Inquisitor." [29] The Grand Inquisitor bestows on millions of people the happiness of servile obedience by withdrawing from them the burden of freedom, which is beyond their strength. Freedom is believed to be a burden which man would be glad to lay on another's shoulders but he must not do so because of his humanity. For Dostoevsky, the denial of the freedom of the spirit is the temptation of anti-Christ. Authoritarianism is based on the principle of anti-Christ. Religious teachers try to convince and not coerce. Authoritarian faiths contain within themselves the seeds of their own decline. For a time they can remove from men's minds the sense of fear, doubt and uncertainty but they cannot produce lasting results. They provide security only so long as our minds are insensitive to other influences.

The authoritarian faiths and atheism which stands at the opposite extreme are both victims of superstition. They deny the free man, the responsible actor. They eliminate initiative and tend to dehumanise man. In extreme forms of totalitarianism, religious and political, there is a tendency to reduce human beings into mechanisms responding to stimuli, puppets twitched into sacrifice and suffering by the dictates of the leaders.[30]

[29] *The Brothers Karamazov;* see also the "Revolutionary Club" in *The Possessed.*

[30] In 1870 when an announcement of a new dogma was made, Lord Acton said that he did not see why he should change his religion because the Pope changed his.

8. DOUBT AND BELIEF

The alternatives to religion we have considered do not remove our anxieties, as they stifle the fears and impart courage by making us members of a collective whole, a political party or a confessional church. They can be overcome only by an active and continuous struggle with doubt and despair. In a crowd we cease to be free persons in full and free encounter with reality. We live in an age bitterly conscious of its inadequacy and seeking wild compensations. When we suffer from acute introspection bordering on a nervous breakdown, any force which offers to stabilise our natures is welcome. Anyone who provides an illusion for our comfort, an idol for our worship, gets a hearing. There is no mental perversion so extreme that it cannot find followers. There is no cause so foolish that men will not die for it. The distressing feature of our age is not its atheism but its belief, the strange forms of superstition which it is willing to adopt. Atheists are many but unbelievers few. The age of faith is always with us; only the object of our faith changes. We depart from one creed only to embrace another. The new cults are built on something which is more fundamental than the desire for truth. It is the desire for faith. However much we may avoid the recognition of that necessity, we need some certainty, some view that will make sense of life and give to it an intelligent and winning goal. These new loyalties are, however, petty and provincial and breed new illusions which result in new catastrophes and produce new waves of cynical world weariness.

Man is never nearer God than in the extremity of his anguish. Then, and not till then, do we hear an echo of that

bitterest of all human cries, "They have taken away the Lord
. . . and we know not where they have laid him." Where
shall we go, to what God shall we make our offering? [31] Who
has the words of eternal life? This imploring cry does not proceed from the lips of the righteous orthodox who are ever sure
of their course and are utterly confident that they have paid
their debts to God. It is the unhappy creatures, who have
passed through the depths of doubt, who have nowhere left to
turn, it is they who are engaged in what Karl Jaspers calls "the
impassioned struggle with God for God." [32] Even the greatest
of us have been liable to nihilistic despair. It is a transitional
stage which earnest spirits cannot evade. In the process of defending God against God, they touch the rock bottom of despair.

We need a philosophy, a direction, and a hope if the present
state of indecision is not to lead us to chaos. The agitation of
minds, all eager for a new light, suggests that we may be on
the boundaries of a new life. We are in search of a religious
message that is distinctive, universally valid, sufficient and
authoritative, one that has an understanding of the fresh sense
of truth and the awakened social passion which are the prominent characteristics of the religious situation today. Belief may
be difficult but the need for believing is inescapable. We must
present struggling and aspiring humanity with a rational faith,
which does not mock the free spirit of man by arbitrary dogmas or hesitating negations, a new vision of God in whose
name we can launch a crusade against the strange cults which
are now competing for mastery over the souls of men.

[31] kasmai devāya haviṣā vidhema?
[32] *The Perennial Scope of Philosophy,* Eng. translation (1950), p. 43.
See also Ecclesiastes.

4

The Quest for Reality

I. SCIENTIFIC APPROACH

ALL religious thinkers offer proofs for the existence of God. We find them in the Upaniṣads and Buddhism, in Plato and Aristotle. St. Thomas Aquinas' five proofs are well known.* Kant bases his theistic conviction on the nature of human conscience and Hegel on the nature of human knowledge. Religion should satisfy our instinct for truth. God is truth. He is *satyasvarūpa*. He is of the nature of truth. Gandhi used to say that Truth is God and not God is Truth. This statement is a commentary on the Upaniṣad text, *tapo brahma*. Sincere and reverent thinking is itself divine. The Buddha insists that reason based on evidence is our only guide to truth. He asks us not to believe any sacred book because of its antiquity or regard for its author. Each one should search for himself, think for himself and realise for himself. Jesus affirms that the spirit of truth is in us and it will make us free.[1] When Jesus asks us to love God with our whole being, he means that we should love him with intelligence which is the principal part of our being. What is required of us is intelligent, not sentimental love.

* Cf. *Approaches to God,* by Jacques Maritain, *World Perspectives,* Vol. I.
[1] John 14:17.

Where the spirit of the Lord is, there is liberty, liberty to
think and act freely. In all circumstances, truth is more valuable than its opposite. Even if truth comes to us in a form that
seems strange to us, that makes difficulties for us, that requires
surrender of our cherished beliefs, the final result can never be
injury to the human spirit or the good of the world. The story
of man's pilgrimage is a perpetual quest for truth, searching,
finding and setting forth to search again. It is thus that we
grow and enlarge our experience. Whether we are scientists or
religious men we are committed unreservedly to the search
for truth. Science is not sentiment, nor is religion dogma. The
truth which science offers us will make for greater depth in
religion.[2]

It is against the spirit of truth if science assumes an authority
over mind, giving up its proper function of a method of inquiry. It becomes a superstition, if it frees its votaries from the
duty of independent thought. About the middle of the nineteenth century, science became as dogmatic as any religious
hypothesis. It assumed that the world and everything within it
was an elaborate mechanism in which everything was resolv-
able at last into hard material particles. Such a mechanist interpretation excluded any genuine possibility of the rise of the
values of mind and spirit.

The mechanist view is not a fact of science but a finding of
the scientist. Communism, for example, professes to be based

[2] Albert Schweitzer has expressed this forcibly: "If thought is to set
out on its journey unhampered, it must be prepared for anything, even
for arrival at intellectual agnosticism. But even if our will-to-action is
destined to wrestle endlessly and unavailingly with an agnostic view of
the universe and of life, still this painful disenchantment is better for it
than persistent refusal to think out its position at all. For this disenchantment does, at any rate mean that we are clear as to what we are
doing." *Decay and Restoration of Civilisations* (1947), p. 104.

on science and proclaims that there is no God. Science does not justify this claim. It does not prove or disprove the reality of God any more than it proves or disproves the beauty of the sunset or the greatness of Hamlet.

There are two sides to scientific activity, the discovery of facts and the construction of an intellectual pattern which will explain them, taking into account other known facts. While facts are established, interpretations are provisional. Again, facts are not judgments of value. When we attempt to interpret facts as a whole and pronounce judgments on their meaning and value, we get beyond science. The scientific mind is satisfied with secondary causes; the philosophical mind demands final causes. An infinite series of causes is no explanation.

Like philosophy, religion is an attempt to account for our experience as a whole. Experience is of different kinds. It relates to the world of objects, of nature studied by the natural sciences; the world of individual subjects, their thoughts and feelings, desires and decisions, studied by the social sciences, psychology and history; and the world of values, studied by literature, philosophy and religion. We should interpret these different types of experience and frame a consistent pattern to guide us. Our concepts of nature, soul and God die if they have no roots in experience. In the interpretation of experience, we employ methods of reason. It is the only way of attaining truth. A proposition cannot be true for religion and false for reason. The Thomistic idea maintains that truth is one and apparently contradictory views are capable of reconciliation. All the thirsts of the spirit, including the thirst for the knowledge of the truth, need to be satisfied. When we were unable to understand the world and lived at the mercy of natural forces whose workings were beyond our knowledge and control, we peopled the world with gods and goddesses of our own imagining, spirits, good and evil, who could be propitiated and won over. As our knowledge of nature increased, we became proud of our achievements in science and assumed that science would be able to envisage and explain all that has happened and all that will happen in terms of "the ultimately purely natural and inevitable march of evolution from the atoms of the primaeval nebula to the proceedings of the British Association for the Advancement of Science." [3] Whereas, in the first stage, reality was treated as something given and unchangeable and man's duty was conceived to be one of submission to reality and to the conditions that it imposed, in the second stage, man's capacity to subdue reality to the pattern of his desires and make it conform to his wishes was recognised. In the first stage, there was greater stress on man's control of himself and submission to nature; in the second greater stress on the technical control over matter. In the first, the need for acquiring wisdom and self-control was prominent; in the second, the need for acquiring knowledge which will enable man to control his environment was stressed.

The old belief which was current even a few decades ago that if scientific research were given free play, superstition would be destroyed and mystery exposed and man would become master not only of the world but of himself has been given up even by the scientists, who approach their task in a spirit of humility, conscious that before the wonders and mysteries of the world, man is an ignorant being knowing not whence he comes or whither he goes. Scientists are not certain that they know anything for certain. Every advance in knowl-

[3] Professor Tyndall in his presidential address to the British Association for the Advancement of Science in 1874.

edge reveals a greater unknown. It does not answer the vital questions whether existence has any meaning, whether life makes sense, whether rightness is inherent in the nature of things. Kant, who attested his reverence for the cosmic order, felt that natural laws had little to say about value or obligation. For him there was a kingdom of ends which was ordered according to an inviolable moral law even as the empirical world is by the laws of nature. Ludwig Wittgenstein acknowledges the undemonstrability of ultimate values by objective science. He says: "We feel that even if all possible scientific questions were answered, our vital problems are not yet touched." [4] Life is larger than science and the human quest is a many-sided one.

Simply because we believe in reason, it does not follow that we should not recognise a mystery when we meet one.[5] Only in the statement of this mystery we should not suffer a conflict between what is reasonably regarded as established knowledge and religious truth. Belief in the religious reality may not be capable of logical proof but belief in it may be shown to be reasonable. Reason itself may take us from the realm of law or science to the realm of wonder, mystery or religion.

The most obvious fact of life is its transitoriness, its perishableness. Everything in the world passes away, the written word, the carved stone, the painted picture, the heroic act. Our thoughts and acts, our deeds of glory, our economic arrangements, our political institutions, our great civilisations are a part of history, subject to the law of time. The earth on

[4] *Tractatus logico-philosophicus*, 6, 52.
[5] Cf. J. E. C. McTaggart: "[There is] a mysticism which starts from the understanding and only departs from it insofar as that standpoint shows itself to be not ultimate, but to postulate something beyond itself." *Studies in Hegelian Cosmology* (1901), p. 292.

G

which we live may one day become unfit for human habitation as the sun ages and alters. All things belong to the world of becoming, of process, of time. Existence and transitoriness are interchangeable.[6]

In all forms of Indian thought, time is symbolised by birth and death. The world is represented by the wheel of time, of births and deaths. The question for philosophy is whether this all-devouring time, this saṁsāra is all or whether there is anything else beyond time. Is this world, this perpetual procession of events self-maintaining, self-sustaining, self-established or is there a beyond, underlying it, standing behind it, inspiring it, holding it together?

Before we attempt to answer this question, we should note the central features of this world process. The most obvious characteristic is its orderedness. The cosmic process is not an unintelligible chaos. It is governed by certain fixed laws. We can plan and predict, learn from experience, gain dependable knowledge and seek future ends. There is no interference with nature's settled order and so we are able to understand the laws which govern the world. If the universe were lawless, if the sun's rise and the seed's growth happened in a haphazard way, the world could hardly go on and our life would become a nightmare. The world is not bereft of sense. There is a law, a pattern according to which things move. Many of the great thinkers like Newton and Kant were impressed by the sublimity of the cosmic order.

It follows that the natural calamities which sometimes occa-

[6] "As for man, his days are as grass
As a flower of the field, so he flourisheth.
For the wind passeth over it, and it is gone
And the place thereof shall know it no more." Psalm 103: 15, 16.
"Death is the horizon of being." Heidegger.

sion great distress are also the results of the working of laws. If miracles should happen to thwart the results of the operation of natural laws, knowledge and reasonable conduct would become impossible. Nature has a rhythm of her own and this is essential for man's life.

The world is not a mere repetition of order; it makes advances into the future. In the cosmic process we notice the emergence of a series of levels of being each obeying its own laws, yet constituting an advance on the preceding members of the series. An early Upaniṣad, the *Taittirīya,* mentions five levels of reality in the cosmic process, *anna* or matter, *prāṇa* or life, *manas* or animal mind, *vijñāna* or human intelligence and *ānanda* or spiritual freedom.[7] These are qualitatively distinct. Each level has its own governing principles or laws peculiar to it. The laws of the higher level do not displace those of the lower but add something new or qualitatively distinct to them. Even the theory of dialectical idealism (Hegel) or materialism (Marx) admits the fact of advance. History is a forward movement and not an endless recurrence or repetition. The aim of the universe, for the Upaniṣad, is to produce beings in whom mind (*manas*) and intellect (*vijñāna*) shall lead to spiritual excellence (*ānanda*). When the Kingdom of the Spirit, *brahma-loka* as it is called, is established we have the triumph and the fulfilment of the cosmic process. The promise of this Kingdom of God is given to us in the God-men, Buddha, Zoroaster, Socrates, Jesus.

Christian doctrine looks upon the world as a preparation for the Kingdom of God. This world is the training ground for mankind to attain perfection. Even Herbert Spencer had faith

[7] Lloyd Morgan suggests the following steps: atom, molecule, colloidal unit, cell, multicellular organism, and society of organisms.

in the divine consummation for the world. "The ultimate development of the ideal man is certain—as certain as any conclusion in which we place the most implicit faith, for instance, that all men die." For him "progress is not an accident but a necessity. What we call evil and immorality must disappear." "It is certain that man must become perfect." Samuel Alexander tells us that space-time, the matrix from which the cosmos has evolved, develops by the inner necessity of its own being ever higher stages of consciousness. It has developed human beings and will develop god-men. Whitehead, with his conception of God as "the completed ideal harmony," looks upon the purpose of the cosmos as "the attainment of value in the temporal world."

Any philosophic attempt should comprehend the various spheres of the inorganic, the organic, etc., in one scheme of interpretation. It should take into account the fact of the world process, its orderedness, its development. The qualities of existence, order, development, purposefulness demand an ontological foundation.

Why is there existence? Why is there anything at all? If everything disappeared there would be utter nothingness. If that nothingness did not provide or was not itself the possibility of being, there could not have been anything at all. The existences of the world are imperfect and impermanent and nothing that is imperfect can subsist of itself or by itself for insofar as it is imperfect it is not. The Upaniṣads lead us from the imperfect existences in the world to the Supreme and Absolute Being which is on every side, beneath, above, beyond, whose centre is everywhere, even in the smallest atom, and whose circumference is nowhere, as it spreads beyond all measure. The existence of the world means the primacy of

Being. The very fact that becoming comes to be, that it has a beginning means that there is something that has not itself become. The root principle is not the primordial night of nothingness but is Absolute Being. Being denotes pure affirmation to the exclusion of every possible negation. It is absolute self-absorbed Being, the one Supreme Identity beyond existence and non-existence, the universal reality. When Moses asked God, after the latter had sent him to Egypt to save his brethren: "If they should say to me, what is his name? What shall I say to them?" God replied to him: "You will tell them, 'I am who am.' " [8]

There would be no existence, no becoming, no manifestation at all, if there were not non-being. Without non-being, Being would be mere self-identity and there would be no manifestation, no expression. It is non-being that drives Being from its immovable self-identity and enables it to express itself. It is non-being that reveals God as power. No revelation is possible without the ground of Being and the principle of non-being. When we say that something *is,* we mean that it participates in Being but is not identical with Being.

Being itself is viewed as pure subject faced by non-subject, pure self as against non-self. Being is now the personal God moving on the waters of non-being. Being is the Supreme Self, *Īśvara* conscious of non-being, *prakṛti, māyā* which he controls. He is self and not-self, Ahura-Mazdā, the lord of life and the creator of matter. Śamkara says that all things are of the nature of Being—non-being, *sad-asad-ātmaka.* Boehme ex-

[8] Exodus 3:13–14. Father Heras, deciphering the Mohenjo Daro Inscriptions, says: "The self subsistence of God is evident from the name of God, Iruvan, 'The one who exists.' " "The Religion of Mohenjo Daro People According to the Inscriptions," *Journal of the University of Bombay,* Vol. V, p. 3.

pressed it by saying that all things are rooted in a *yes* and a *no*. The process of the universe is a perpetual overcoming of non-being by Being. Being therefore includes non-being within itself. In the creative universe, Being affirms itself and over-comes its own non-being.

Non-being is dependent on the Being it negates. The very word non-being indicates the ontological priority of Being over non-being. There could be no non-being if there were not a preceding Being. The personal God is the first determination from which flow all other determinations. Being embraces it-self and that which is opposed to it, non-being. Non-being belongs to Being. It cannot be separated from it. When it is said that God has power, it means that Being will overcome the resistance of non-being. It affirms itself against non-being. Hegel makes out that negation is the power driving the Abso-lute Idea towards existence and driving existence back towards the Absolute Idea which, in the process, actualises itself as Absolute Mind or Spirit.

We know that this universe *is;* we know that it has a par-ticular character. But why is the universe what it is and not something else? Why is there this universe rather than another? If this universe were an organic expression of the Divine Being and Consciousness, the Divine would be subjected to the forms of this universe. It would not be the free choice of the Divine from out of a boundless realm of possibilities. If it were a free choice of the Divine, it means that the Divine Creativity is not bound up with this world in such a way that the changes of this world affect the integrity of the Divine. God is absolute freedom for he is from himself, *a se.* This world is the expres-sion of freedom, of the joy of the Supreme.

The world is not an accident or a contingency in the sense

that it is causally undetermined. Freedom means that the de-
termining cause has no ultimate necessity. It is given; it cannot be logically derived from the nature of the Supreme. We
may call it the irrationality, or the mystery of the freedom of
the Supreme. Aristotle makes out that there could be no
motion in the universe without the presence of God, who is
the mover; he moves only by being an object of appetition to
the world but he remains himself unmoved. The changes
of the world do not affect his nature. Creation is the activity
of self-communication which belongs to God's life.

Hegel identifies the Absolute with the cosmic process. It
makes little difference whether we say that it is spirit that
is realising itself in movement or that matter, moving in
the direction of spirit, becomes conscious of itself. The late
Professor Pringle-pattison, following Hegel, thought that the
world was organic to God and not accidental. The Hegelian
view becomes pantheistic in the sense of a substantial identity
between the metaphysical reality and the manifested world.
Pure Being transcends all duality and thus all secondary expressions of this duality. Nothing can be substantially identical
with the Absolute as pure Being. Even the nature of God is not
exhausted by the world of existence. It is one possibility that is
being accomplished in this cosmic process. When the cosmic
process reaches its goal, it is taken over into the timeless and
spaceless life of the Absolute. The pantheist view takes away
the absoluteness of the Absolute and subjects it to the forms of
the finite.

There is order in the universe and all order is the expression
of a mind and so the universe is the expression of a Supreme
Mind. The adaptation of means to ends which we find in the
world cannot be due to chance. It suggests an ordering and

organising Mind.[9] We do not know how life got into the material world or how mind crept into the world of life. If our experience consists of sense impressions how do we get knowledge? How is it that we put a construction on what our senses receive from the world? What Abt Vogler thinks of music is true of all creation:

> I know not if, save in this, such gift is allowed to man
> That out of three sounds he frame, not a fourth sound but
>   a star.

If philosophy attempts to explain and not merely describe the different stages, it speaks of a nisus (Lloyd Morgan and Alexander) or a trend towards holism (Smuts). It points to a unitary agency which remains the same through its varied manifestations. It expresses itself in the various levels of organisation and culminates in spiritual freedom, which is the goal of the cosmic process. We cannot account for the dynamic and creative character of the universe if the Primary Being is not also creative. Whitehead says that "what men call God— the Supreme God of rationalised religion" is "the actual but non-temporal entity whereby the indeterminateness of mere creativity is transmuted into a determinate freedom." [10]

The cosmic process would be a shapeless chaos, the universe would be an inert mass, if the cosmic principle of order and movement, what the ancient Greeks called the Logos, did not function. The Divine Intelligence is the intermediary between the Absolute Being and the cosmic process. The cosmic order

---

[9] The French physiologist Geley said: "Does not this whole conglomeration of facts, brought to our attention by different scientists, give proof of the extraordinary, amazing, incomprehensible, I would say, miraculous intelligence of life?"

[10] *Science and the Modern World* (1926), p. 90.

and progress are explained by the hypothesis of a living God in action. All initiative in nature and history is due to the working of the Spirit, inspiring the insight of the seers, the knowledge of the wise, the genius of the artist and the skill of the craftsman. The *Bhagavadgītā* tells us: "Whatsoever being there is, endowed with glory and grace and vigour, know that to have sprung from a fragment of My splendour." [11] From the Supreme Spirit come the endowments of all those who wish to inaugurate the reign of God on earth. The real which accounts for the existence of the universe is Being (*sat*), its character which accounts for the ordered advance is consciousness (*cit*) with freedom and joy (*ānanda*).

The question whether the existence of evil and imperfection in this world is compatible with a religious view has been a source of great perplexity to believing minds. Things created have an element of imperfection; if they do not have it, there will be nothing to distinguish God from his creation. Imperfection is an aspect of the existent world. We cannot say that only a world of ease and comfort is consistent with providential government. If the purpose of human life is the shaping of human souls through conflict with evil and pain and conquest over uncertainty and scepticism, this world is not ill adapted for that purpose. The very transitoriness of life imparts value, dignity and charm to it. If the purpose of this life is the emergence of moral and spiritual values, then it cannot be free from pain and difficulties. "Do you not see," wrote Keats in a letter, "how necessary a world of pain and trouble is to school an intelligence and make it a soul." The cross which is the emblem of sorrow and suffering is also the sign of salvation.

God subdues the world to himself. In the end the grossness

[11] X, 41.

of the earth will be taken away and the purpose of God will prevail. This is the *brahma-loka* of the Hindus, the Kingdom of Heaven of the Christians and the Paradise of the Muslims. *Brahma-loka* is not another world than *saṁsāra,* it is the world of *saṁsāra* redeemed. When the Sufi Er Razi said the "Paradise is the prison of the initiate as the world is the prison of the believer," he was making out that Paradise is a limitation or a manifestation of the Supreme Unmanifested Reality. It is a conditioned state, one cosmic reflection of the Unconditioned Being. That which has a beginning has an end even if it lasts for billions of years. History is encompassed by the broader horizon. Time is in eternity.

It is wrong to separate the Kingdom to come from the kingdom of this world. The separation between the two is artificial. Christianity, according to W. R. Inge, does not offer us any hope that, in given time, man must become perfect.[12] Edwyn Bevan asks us to "beware of supposing that it is possible for us to trace any approximation in the course of history to the Kingdom of God. The idea of a progressive approximation came in only with the general idea of evolution in the nineteenth century. . . . The early Church had no thought of such approximation." "It is only the heavenly hope that is essential to Christianity. . . . There can be no assurance that things upon earth will grow any better before the end of history comes."[13] All the time the Christian task is to bring human society into conformity with the divine pattern. If this world is a revelation of the purpose of God, as time goes on, the revelation must be more extensive. St. Paul expects a period of progressive development culminating in the fulfilment of the

[12] *The Idea of Progress* (1920).
[13] *The Kingdom of God and History* (1938), Oxford Conference Series, p. 66.

purpose of creation through agony and travail.[14] Even Inge concedes "that there may be an immanent teleology which is shaping the life of the human race towards some completed development which has not yet been reached." His complaint is against the application of the concept of progress to reality as a whole. In spheres within reality, progress is possible and probable.

Though Professor Arnold Toynbee adopts a cyclic theory of civilisations, he suggests that "the breakdowns and disintegrations of civilisations might be the stepping stones to higher things on the religious plane." [15] The Christian, the Buddhist and the Muslim work in the hope of the evangelisation of mankind to their own beliefs. These as well as the philosophies which believe in a series of ascending levels of emergent or creative evolution accept progress in history. There is a purpose in the cosmic process. We may glimpse what it is and understand the meaning in the apparent confusion by which we are surrounded.

When we work from the cosmic end, we are led to the hypothesis of a Supreme whose nature is Being, Consciousness, Freedom, Power and Goodness. The Absolute is the abode of infinite possibilities and in its creative aspect one of these possibilities is freely chosen for accomplishment. The power of creativity is not alien to Being. It does not enter it from outside. It is in Being, inherent in it. When we stress the creative side, the Supreme Godhead or the Absolute Brahman is called God. Brahman and Īśvara, Godhead and God are one. Brahman refers to infinite being and possibility and Īśvara to creative freedom. This world is presided over by the cosmic

[14] I Corinthians 12:4–27; Romans 12:45; Colossians 2:19. See also Ephesians 4:4–16.
[15] *Civilisation on Trial* (1948), p. 240; also see pp. 25 ff.

Lord (Hiraṇyagarbha), who is the manifestation of Brahman-Īśvara. The world is a *manifestation* of the cosmic Lord and a *creation* of God.[16] The universe is an incarnation in which one Idea of God is made flesh.[17] The unincarnate God has a wider range than the incarnate God. The Absolute Creative God and the Cosmic Lord are not to be regarded as separate entities. They are different ways of viewing the One Transcendent Being.[18] The Incomprehensible at the centre makes all other things coherent and comprehensible. Pure Being is not an abstraction, not a barrenness but is the source of all variety. It is Being in its most concrete form including within itself every manifestation of Being.[19] The world in which we live is subject to change. It is saṁsāra, the stream of existence, the realm of flux and becoming. It is also the place where we have the opportunity of finding the meaning of life. Until we reach the further shore of enlightenment, we have to move in the stream. All things in the world, though unreal and fleeting, contain an element of reality for Being is present in them all.[20] We can live eternally in this world for this world is one of the modes of manifestation of the Absolute.

A brief consideration of the features of this world of existence suggests to us the reality of spirit higher than ourselves

[16] Cf. John 14:28: "For the Father is greater than I."

[17] The word (*logos*) of God operates beyond the historic person of Jesus, from the beginning of creation. John 1:1-11.

[18] See *The Principal Upaniṣads* (1954), pp. 57-68; *The Philosophy of Sarvepalli Radhakrishnan* (1952), pp. 26-47.

[19] The conception of Christian Trinity symbolises a unity that includes a multiplicity.

[20] Cf. F. H. Bradley: "We can find no province of the world so low but the Absolute inhabits it. Nowhere is there even a single fact so fragmentary and so poor that to the universe it does not matter. There is truth in every idea however false, there is reality in every existence however slight: and where we can point to reality or truth, there is the one undivided life of the Absolute." *Appearance and Reality* (1925), p. 487.

whose qualities are not merely majesty and power but love and goodness.

Pure Being which is the Absolute can only be indicated. It can be alluded to but not described. God is regarded as a Supreme Person. He is certainly higher than anything he has created. He is personal but not in the sense in which we define personality. He has all the good qualities which men have but in a different sense. He is good and wise but not good and wise as we are.[21] We may use different names for God but their powers are one and the same.[22]

2. THE HUMAN PREDICAMENT

The universe is not just what the senses aided by the scientific instruments show to us. We must know not only the interior of the atom but also the inner world of man. The precept of the Upaniṣads, know the self, *ātmānam viddhi,* the injunction of the Greeks, "Know thyself," stress the importance of self-knowledge. From early times, religious thinkers tried to detect the vibrations of the individual, explore his secret movements, and follow his obscure preoccupations. Man remains a mystery to himself. Socrates felt it as Plato so impressively shows us in his *Phaedrus.* Man is always more than he is able to comprehend of himself. When he looks upon himself as an object, he is the subject which apprehends and knows itself. Thus man is forever transcending himself. The self goes beyond the perceptions of ideas, realisations of meanings and experiences of suffering and bliss. It is however an illusion to think that the human individual can understand himself as he really is. Plato makes fun of the philosophers who believed that they

[21] The Psalmist says: "Is he deaf, the God who implanted hearing in us; is he blind, the God who gave eyes to see?"
[22] mahad devānām asuratvam ekam. *Ṛg. Veda,* III, 55.

"like the gods can look down on human life from above." [23]

Man is more than a physical being. Psychology is not a mere extension of physiology. There is a part in man's nature which is not merely objective; it is this non-objective aspect which gives man his uniqueness in the world of nature. Man is not merely a creature of instinct, not merely a centre of mind. His nature is not exhausted by that which he becomes as an object of physiology, psychology or sociology.

The different theories advanced for the rise of religious consciousness, the animistic, the magical and the sociological, agree in holding that religion is a device for overcoming man's fear and loneliness. But why have we this fear, this feeling of loneliness? Is the frightened individual the end of the cosmic process or has he another destiny?

For the Indian thinkers, the problem of religion is bound up with man's intellectual nature, his distinctive way of knowing himself and the world in which he lives. Consciousness and choice distinguish men from other species. Consciousness leads to moral responsibility through choice. Man suffers from unawareness (avidyā) which gives rise to selfish desire (kāma). Man is in a stricken or fallen condition. He has slowly evolved from the animal level and has developed self-consciousness which is an unhappy and divided consciousness. The Buddha says that life is suffering. We live in a world governed by karma or necessity.

The symbolism of the Fall [24] expresses the same truth. Man tastes the fruit of the tree of knowledge and the result is his fall. Intellectual knowledge is a leap forward in man's aware-

[23] *Sophist.*
[24] Genesis 2.

ness but is said to be a fall since it produces a fissure or a cleavage in man's life, a break in the natural order. Adam and Eve were smitten with fear the moment they became aware of the new relationship with reality into which they entered by eating of the fruit of the tree of the knowledge of good and evil. They are afraid that they may not rise equal to the sense of obligation which that awareness imposes. Their state is said to be a fallen one, as they search for light as for something lost, which they are able to glimpse dimly. The narrative in Genesis is not to be understood as a literal account of what happened. It is a myth or a symbol contrasting the state of Adam before the Fall and his state after it. The former is God's intention for human life; the latter is his actual life by virtue of the frustration of that intention by man's disobedience.

Every animal is perfect in its own way; it fulfils itself within its life cycle. It is no doubt subject to death but it is not aware of it. It is thought that induces in man the feeling of fear and loneliness, that discloses to him his inadequacy, his need for growth. The dawn of intellectual consciousness marks the end of his elemental state of wholeness and innocence.[25] Man suffers from a sense of insecurity. He is torn, distressed and asks, who shall save me from the body of this death? The uncertainty of life and the instinct for self-preservation get into conflict. What is inertia in the material world, self-preservation in the biological world, becomes at the human level longing for continuance. All beings tend towards preservation or enhancement

[25] "Man is only a reed, the weakest in nature, but he is a thinking reed. It is not necessary for an entire universe to arm itself to crush him, a vapour, a drop of water, is enough to kill him. But, even if the universe crushed him, man would still be more noble than what kills him, because he knows he is dying, and knows the advantage which the universe has over him; the universe knows nothing of it all." Pascal, *Pensées*, 398.

of life. They exert themselves with all the energy of their being against anything which threatens them with destruction. The question is: Will man annihilate death, nothingness, or will nothingness annihilate him?

Striving to mitigate the dread of mortality, man, in every age, has devised formulas and sophistries which relate to far kingdoms where the spirits of the dead are said to dwell forever. Even the Neanderthal man buried his dead. The idea of final extinction was unbearable to him. The dead are not dead. There is a beyond where the dead live. They will wake up and feel hungry. They will have to adorn themselves, defend themselves. So food, pigments for colouring the body, ornaments and weapons accompany the deceased. When our dear ones are taken from us, we enshrine their memories in our hearts and believe that they live in another realm. Death is rebirth into another sphere, we assume.

For Plato, philosophy is a meditation on death. For Heidegger, metaphysics starts with the realisation that man suffers from "a radical insecurity of being." He is thrown into the world to which he clings forgetting that it is nought. That we can be at home in the world is the great illusion. For Heidegger, all existence is infected with the character of time, of historicity. It is threatened with two dreadful convictions, that of death and transitoriness,[26] and the dread of death. Man, says Heidegger, is aware of the intense actuality of life at the moment life is ebbing away. Is it possible, asks Heidegger, that time, despite its ontological nature and all the consequences

[26] Nicolas Berdyaev writes: "I would never be reconciled to the fact that time is in a perpetual flux and that each moment is devoured by, and vanishes into, the succeeding one. This terrible aspect of time has caused me intense and unspeakable pain. To part with people, with things, with places, has been a source of agony to me as dreadful as death." *Dream and Reality* (1950), p. 29.

that follow from it, offers us a ground for our existence and a certainty that will permit us to gain a fundamental tranquillity of soul? "Temporality discloses itself as the meaning of real dread (*Sorge*)." Human experience is laden with care. In the exciting moments of fear, in the devastating experience of being thrown into the world of space and time, man finds that he stands on the obscure ground of a mysterious nothing, which is not a mere mathematical zero but something more positive than that; when man experiences this "nothingness" in all its existential weight, he suffers from a feeling of profound unrest and care, a "radical insecurity of being." This encounter with non-existence, this fear of nothingness is not so much a metaphysical concept as a psychological state, an inner condition which provokes the sense of dread and starts the religious quest. Deliverance from the illusions of this world is to be achieved only by facing nothingness and overcoming it.

Self-consciousness implies ethical freedom. Human beings are original, unique, creative spirits who are not bound by the necessities of the space-time world. To say that man has freedom is to affirm that he has an element which is not inescapably subject to regulation by another. The subject is superior to the object. Eternity expresses itself in free decisions in time. By the employment of freedom, man can raise himself to the divine status or degrade himself into animal life. He can stretch to infinity or shrink into insignificance. If we are created automata bound to act virtuously, there is no virtue in our conduct. When it is possible for us to act wrongly, if we act rightly there is merit.

For man, to live means to give existence to the possible. Every moment we literally make ourselves by choosing from the future, which is the realm of the possible. Whenever we

H

live creatively we overcome the force of non-being and affirm the Being in us. In every act of creative freedom we try to become what we potentially are, to actualise the Being in us. A free choice is liberation from servitude. It is not continuous with the past. It is a leap, not a development. Man exists because he has freedom. To exist is to stand out of the crowd, to be oneself, to be an authentic purpose making and remaking oneself. Man has no nature but has a history. For Sartre, the human being is sharply distinguished from the world of things. Things are merely what they are. They are completely self-subsistent. In his language, a thing is an *en-soi,* something in itself. Man alone is *pour-soi,* for himself. He has the dignity of a cause, in the words of Thomas Aquinas.

Man's free will is the source of selfish ambition as well as of disinterested love. While the true law of his being is love, a relation of harmony with all living beings, he often rebels against this law. A defiant self-affirmation which leads to self-enslavement, an abuse of freedom which destroys itself, overtakes him. The possibility of the misuse of freedom becomes an actuality. Freedom is used to develop wilfulness which breeds evil. To be good is to be capable of all evil and yet commit none. Evil is not a necessary result of freedom. It is the result of its abuse. The fault is not in our gods or our stars but in ourselves. We are responsible beings, who can, if we will, choose the right and reject the wrong. We are not the victims of external forces that bind our bodies or control our souls.

When, according to Euripedes in his *Troades* (983–97), Helen defends her conduct by making herself out to have been the helpless victim of Aphrodite, Hecuba rejects this plea and declares that the beauty of Paris and the prospect of wealth and luxury with him in Troy made Helen choose de-

liberately to go off with him. "It was not Cypris," says Hecuba
to Helen, "but your own heart, that made you yield to Paris."

Man has the knowledge of good and evil. Insofar as he is
human, he must do either good or evil. If he drifts without
using his freedom, submitting to automatism, he ceases to be
man. It is better to do evil than to surrender to routine for we
then assert our humanity.

The fact of freedom, according to Kierkegaard, produces
anxiety, the fear that we may abuse our freedom. While the
fact of freedom places man above the animals, it fills him at
the same time with anxiety or dread (*angst*). He is aware of
the possibility of a fall for he knows, within his soul, there are
dis-relationships within his own nature and in relation to the
Power that constitutes it. Kierkegaard calls these dis-relationships despair, "sickness unto death." For Sartre, man is what
he wills: "He is nothing else but that which he makes of himself." When Sartre says that "the essence of man is his existence," he makes out that there is no essential nature of man.
He makes what he is but does not find it. Man is what he
makes of himself. This is essential Buddhism. When *Advaita
Vedānta* speaks of an eternal unchanging self, this is the Universal Self which is non-participating. The individual self is
perpetually changing. Nothing is in man which is not by man.

Sartre refers to the fact of human freedom and builds a
philosophy of despair on it. When we arrive in this world we
are compelled to choose. We are condemned to be free. Sartre
protests against every form of determinism and affirms that
man is absolute freedom in the sense that every act is absolutely
original. It does not depend on any motive and is not linked
with the past, and finds its sole justification in man's continu-
ing projection of himself into the future. Man is a law unto

himself. He did not elect to be free. He is fated to be free. We are in anguish because we have to decide. This anguish, according to Sartre, becomes heavier when we realise that each one of us chooses not only for himself but for all. Every free act of each individual is a commitment on behalf of all. The self is not alone but is involved in a network of relationships with others. For Jaspers we are in this world as selves in communication. For Sartre our choices are significant only insofar as they are not momentary but are sustained and become an essential part of our being. We should make no choices which we do not think appropriate to all other selves, who are or might be situated in like positions. All this reminds us of Kant's principle that one should only act as if every action were the basis of a universal law, binding on all men.

Man suffers intellectually from a sense of insecurity, ethically from a sense of anxiety. In moments of self-analysis, he examines his past and feels distressed in spirit, unsure of himself, pulled this way and that. He becomes embittered, sick unto death. He is haunted with a sense of mystery, has the feeling of being weak, incompetent, frail, ignorant, evil, unholy. This unhappy being, whose heart is torn by secret sufferings, is terribly alone, struggling not with external forces but with himself.[27] This divided, riven being, tormented by fear, at odds with himself, is weighed down by despair. There is no unhappiness greater than that of division.

Pascal's words are well-known, "What a chimaera then is man! What a novelty! What a monster, what a chaos, what a contradiction, what a prodigy! Judge of all things, imbecile, worm of the earth; depository of truth, a sink of uncertainty and error; the pride and refuse of the universe."

[27] *Pensées,* 434.

Man's self-consciousness, knowledge of good and evil, freedom and anxiety, which are the symptoms of non-being, these make him yearn for spiritual safety and security, harmony and courage which are the results of the conquest of Being over non-being. Awareness of non-being produces fear, anxiety and discord, and these states, which belong to the structure of human consciousness, are evidence of the non-being which seeks to be overcome by Being. The thirst for religion, the striving for integrality, the search for a different life show that man has to advance by way of consciousness. He must reach out beyond the frontiers of the dual, divided consciousness. The sense of Godforsakenness is itself the witness to the presence of the Divine. The precariousness of this world points to the world beyond. There is a longing for life eternal in the midst of time.

Owing to the delusions of self-conscious intellect and misuse of freedom comes the fall. The way to redemption is to rise to the spirit above reason and the right use of freedom expressing itself in a spontaneous adherence to the law of love. There is a reality that is deeper than the structure of reason. It is at the core of man's being and it enables him to transcend the natural. We are seekers, pilgrims who have no abiding city on earth; we are ever on the move for the city that is to be. It is the pressure of reality that provokes the disquiet in us. The Upaniṣad says: "Lead me from the unreal to the real; lead me from darkness, to light, lead me from death to immortality." [28] The Psalmist says: "Out of the depths I cry to Thee." It is the tension that makes human life so interesting. Eckhart says: "The Soul's perfection consists in liberation from the life that is in part and in admission to the life which is whole. We be-

[28] *Bṛhad-āraṇyaka Upaniṣad*, I, 3, 28.

seech thee, Lord God, to help us escape from the life that is divided into the life that is united." [29]

The human self is not the actual self. It is the possible self, what the self ought to become and can become. Alongside the self as a knowable fact, there is the self as possibility, the spiritual self into which the actual can grow. Man is not merely an object of scientific knowledge. He is immersed in Being. He participates in the creative intuition of the cosmos.[30] The self is cured, according to Kierkegaard, of the sickness of despair and restored to health and wholeness when "by relating itself to its own self, the self is grounded transparently in the power which constituted it." Without freedom there is no possibility of the reintegration of the personality. Man's immediate awareness of freedom has a validity that cannot be undermined by scientific arguments. The awareness of freedom is necessarily associated with a sense of the spiritual reality transcending the world of space and time.

Human nature has immeasurable potentialities and the world process has no predestined goal. The power of free choice gives us hope for the future. We can remake the world. Whatever flaws of character or deficiencies of mind we have we can remove them. If we strive to do so, the forces of the universe will assist us. We can consciously direct the process of human evolution. Nature comes to its fulfilment in the human

[29] Evans, Eng. translation, I, p. 207.

[30] Philostratus in his *Life of Apollonius* (III, 18) records that Apollonius once came across two learned men from India and asked them, "Do you know yourselves?" The two Hindus replied, "If we know everything, it is because first we know ourselves. We would never have succeeded in acquiring wisdom had we not first acquired this self-knowledge." Apollonius, astonished at their reply, inquired further: "What do you think you are?" "We are gods," they replied. And he said, "Why?" "For we are good men," was their answer. "By good deeds we obtain union with God."

individual, who is the bearer of the creative process. He is the unique representative of the universe in whom the unconscious creativity of nature becomes conscious creativity. The inner discord means that he can contend with the disruptive forces, conquer them and attain peace. Human beings cannot remain for long within an impermeable solitude which holds them prisoners of their own anguished desires. The discord is a stage, not the terminus. It is there to be vanquished. It is the symbol of the unsolved tension between hope and fulfilment.

Indian thought asks us to liberate ourselves from bondage. We must pass from saṁsāra, life in time subject to discords to mokṣa or enlightenment or eternal life. Until we reach the unitive life we will have opportunities. The doctrine of saṁsāra governed by the law of karma stresses that each being has many chances to achieve his goal. Each person is the result of his actions and attitudes which he can modify by the exercise of his will.

Until we reach the end of our journey we are subject to the law of karma which makes out that our desires and acts determine the pace of our progress. Our present state is conditioned by our past and what we do now will determine our future. Death and rebirth do not interrupt this process. For our present condition, we are ourselves responsible. We need not blame God or our parents or the existing social order.[31] Even as we are responsible for what we are, we can make ourselves into what we shall be. We are not doomed to continue in our present condition. If we have courage and determination, we can

[31] *Mahābhārata* says that there is no external judge who punishes us; our inner self is the judge.

na yamam yamaḥ ity āhuḥ ātmā vai yama ucyate
ātmā samyamɪto yena yamas tasya karoti kim?

mould our future into a new pattern. Karma is not fatalism.[32]
If we are sincere in our intentions and earnest in our efforts, it
does not matter whether we succeed or not. Whatever advance
we make is not without worth. Whatever the outward results
may be, inner betterment is achieved.

The content of the future is contingent. We can create significance, value, truth, beauty, or their opposites. The responsibility for this is man's and so human freedom posits the reality
of something beyond nature, and nature cannot be absurd or
meaningless for it makes possible the creation of values. There
is a moral order in the world and each man is responsible for
his deeds. His insight and character will grow steadily until
he attains perfection. This doctrine of a succession of opportunities for improving our knowledge and characters, which
is one of the central principles of the Hindu, the Buddhist,
the Jain religions, found followers among the adherents of
other religions, ancient Celts and Teutons, many Jewish and
Muslim mystics, some early Christian Fathers and later heretics. Pythagoras, Empedocles, Plato, Plotinus and Lessing believed in the gradual progress of the individual through many
lives. Kant argues that as the ideal of a harmony between perfect virtue and happiness cannot be realised in one life we can
reach the goal in a successive approach of infinite progression.

The sense of insecurity arising from the contingency of circumstances and the contemplation of death which dissolves the
self, of anxiety arising from the liability to error and sin, of discord and unrest due to a sense of the emptiness and meaning-

[32] Buddha says: "O priests, if any one says that a man *must* reap according to his deeds, in that case there is no religious life, nor is any
opportunity afforded for the entire extinction of suffering. But if any one
says that the reward a man reaps accords with his deeds, in that case
there is a religious life and opportunity is afforded for the entire extinction of suffering."*Anguttara Nikāya,* III, 99, 1.

lessness of life, the sense of fall bears witness to the divine in man which is struggling to become wholly manifest in his awakened consciousness. His alienation from the ground of his being, his unawareness (*avidyā*) has to be replaced by awareness (*vidyā*). This is not purely intellectual. The rebellion against the divine in us is the cardinal sin. Man is ignorant and from ignorance evil ensues.

While the study of the cosmic process leads us to the reality of a Supreme Transcendent God who is the absolutely other, the analysis of human experience brings God near to man. If God and the human soul were completely different, no amount of logical reasoning or mediation could lead us to the reality of God. God-consciousness is as much an original endowment of human beings as self-consciousness. There are degrees of God-consciousness even as there are degrees of self-consciousness. In many men it is dim and confused; only in the redeemed souls is it completely manifest.

3. RELIGION AS EXPERIENCE OF REALITY

When we consider the empirical data of the world and of the human self, we are led to the idea of a Supreme who is Pure Being and Free Activity, who dwells in the inmost self of man. So long as we argue from given data, objective and subjective, it may be said that the Supreme is a necessity of thought, a hypothesis however valid it may be. Articulation in thought of the nature of Ultimate Reality is quite different from experience of it. An idea remains a stranger in the mind, however friendly our reception of it may be, until it receives the stamp of our endorsement by personal experience. Logical arguments by themselves may not be able to demonstrate the existence of God in a way that would satisfy the seeking mind and the devout heart. They indicate the idea, determine its content and state its function in man's inner economy. But there is an ancient and widespread tradition that we can apprehend the Supreme Reality with directness and immediacy. Many people separated by distance of time and space have borne personal testimony to the experience of the Supreme Being, which humbles, chastens and transports us. This direct experience is what Thomas Aquinas calls *cognitio dei experimentalis*.

Everything is known to us only through experience. Even such an abstract science as mathematics is based on the experience of stated regularities. Philosophy of religion must base itself on religious experiences. The existence of God means the real or the possible experience of this Being. If the genuine standard of knowledge is experience, we must deny the character of knowledge to our ideas of God unless they are traced to the experience of God.

An ancient Sanskrit verse says that the assertion of the reality of God is indirect knowledge, the experience of the reality of God is direct knowledge.[33] I am Brahman, *aham brahmāsmi* of the Vedic seers, Jesus' words concerning his divinity, I am the Truth, *ana al-Ḥaqq* of Al Ḥallāj, have a family resemblance. Thomas Aquinas speaks of "knowledge through connaturality." There are two ways of judging things pertaining to a moral virtue, say, courage or fortitude. One may have a theoretical, conceptual or rational knowledge of these virtues but himself be lacking in them. Another possesses the virtues in question in his own powers of will and desire, has them embodied in himself and is connatural with them in his own being. Even so we may have a knowledge of divine reality

[33] asti brahma iti ced veda parokṣam jñānam eva tat
aham brahma iti ced veda pratyakṣam jñānam asti tat

through theology and knowledge of divine reality by personal experience.[34] As the Pseudo-Dionysius put it, we not only learn the truth but suffer it. Kierkegaard's hostility to Hegel was due to the latter's conception of truth as an elaborate speculative system claiming objective validity. For Kierkegaard, truth is to be obtained not by intellectual effort but by personal commitment. Spiritual truth is inwardness, not logical mediation. Truth is existential. To know it we must live in it. It must become a part of our being, a source of personal depth. When Kierkegaard says that subjectivity is truth, he does not mean that man is the measure of all things. He means that truth is not truth until the seeker personally appropriates it.

Spiritual apprehension insists on a participation of the knowing subject in the spiritual reality, a touching (*haptus*) and tasting (*gustus*) of the object of knowledge. We see, feel and taste the truth. This is the immediate awareness of Being itself. It is experience by participation, by a renewal of the self. We apprehend it with all sides of our being, *sarvabhāvena*. Jesus defines the first Commandment thus: "Hear, O Israel: The Lord our God, the Lord is One; and you shall love the Lord your God with all your heart, and with all your soul, and with all your mind and with all your strength." [35] Truth is the vision of reality which satisfies one's whole being. It is grasped by the complete man.

This direct experience is as old as humanity and is not limited to any one race or religion. The intimations of this type of experience are to be found not only in the realms of metaphysics and religion but also in art and communion with nature. In great love, in creative art, in philosophic endeavour, in

[34] *Summa Theologica*, II–II, 45, 2; I, 1, 6, ad 3.
[35] Mark 12:29–30.

moments of intense joy and acute suffering, in the presence of truth, beauty and goodness, we are lifted out of detailed contact with the world of change and succession into an experience of unity and permanence. In these moments of insight in which subject and object are fused into an undifferentiated state, we enter a region beyond love and hate, where the limits of earthly experience fade away and time stands still. There is a world of light beyond the earthly shadows, where the obstinate questionings of the mind are answered and the troubles of the heart are allayed. To experience this reality, to live in it is mokṣa or life eternal. It is release from finitude, fragmentariness, distractedness, unawareness, bondage. It is to be born again, to live in a condition of joy and holy healthfulness.

Mokṣa, Nirvāṇa, the Kingdom of God are not to be pictured as subsequent to or far off from our present existence. The Kingdom of Heaven is not a place of rest after death, something which will someday come on earth. It is a change of consciousness, an inner development, a radical transformation. Spiritual freedom is the power by which we can transcend the world and yet transform it. Here and now we can attain life eternal.

The modern mind with its naturalistic outlook is inclined to treat with scepticism and incredulity cases of conversion and renewal. But rebirth or renewal is not supernatural or unnatural. It is the logical result of the conviction that there is another order of reality interpenetrating the order of this world and continually functioning in it to restore and renovate, to direct and illuminate.

Because the experience is based on immediate intuition, it does not follow that it is invalid. The intuition is supported by reason and does not contradict it. Wisdom and knowledge go together. As the *Bhagavadgītā* puts it, we aim at *jñānam vijñānasahitam*. The truths of the Upaniṣads are the fruits of contemplation and yet they are logically presented. The Upaniṣads emphasize *mīmāṁsā* or investigation.

The concept of personality as a bundle of faculties, intellect, and intuition, desire and will, instinct and emotion is a misleading one. There are no such separate faculties. They shade off one into another by imperceptible gradations. We can distinguish between intellect and intuition in thought but cannot separate them in reality. In all knowledge the whole of our personality is at work. Its different powers are brought into exercise in relation to different kinds of objects. When Plato says only the perfectly real can be perfectly known, he means that the whole personality and not merely the intellect is employed in the knowledge of the "real." Different powers of our minds are used when we attempt to know the familiar order of physical things or the nature of the spiritual world. Science deals with the natural order of events while philosophy and religion speak to us of the order of spirit.

Intellect and integral insight are related as part to whole. Integral insight discloses to us eternity, timelessness in which time and history are included. Truth is not the reflection of reality in sense and intellect. It is a creative mystery experienced by the soul in its deepest being. It is not a question of the subject knowing the object. It involves the realisation that subject and object are one in a deeper sense than any physical analogy can make clear.[36]

In persons of peculiar mental disposition spiritual experience

[36] Eckhart says: "The knower and the known are one. Simple people imagine that they should see God, as if he stood there and they here. This is not so, God and I, we are one in knowledge."

is accompanied by great emotion and attended with unusual phenomena such as swoons and ecstasies, automatic voices and visions. Several other experiences are also permeated by strong emotion. All works of inspiration are by men who feel like possessed beings,[37] but emotional excitement is not enough. This experience is not pathological, though it may happen to accompany certain morbid states. The great seers are mentally healthy. The nervous disturbances which may develop sometimes are merely accidental. The passage from the static to the dynamic, from ignorance to knowledge is a shock to the mental system. We cannot upset the usual relation of the conscious to the unconscious without a risk to the organism. The sudden breaking down of barriers, the exaltation of the mind may disturb mental equilibrium. Transports, raptures, delirium, frenzy, these are not the essentials of spiritual experience. They may arise from spurious sources. The real blessing is not the thrill but the experience of reality.

What is creative about spiritual experience is not its psychological accompaniments but the inward change which manifests itself in the fruits of the spirit, peace, joy, vital vigilance and loving-suffering. A new type of life emerges with a higher

[37] Plato in his *Ion* says: "The epic poets, all the good ones, utter their beautiful poems not from art, but because they are inspired and possessed. So it is also with the good lyric poets; as the worshipping Corybantes are not in their senses when they dance, so the lyric poets are not in their senses when they are composing their lovely strains. . . . A poet is a light and winged thing, and holy, and there is no invention in him until he has become inspired, and is out of his senses, and reason is no longer in him. So long as he has not attained to this state, no man is able to make poetry or to chant in prophecy." 534.

In *Phaedrus* he writes: "He who, having no touch of the Muses' madness in his soul, comes to the doors of poetry, trusting to enter in, and who thinks forsooth that art is enough to make him a poet, remains outside, a bungler; sound reason fades into nothingness before the poetry of madmen." 245.

correspondence between one's self and the ultimate sources of reality. This experience has a functional value in that it fuses all the deep-lying powers of the self, intellect, emotion and will and integrates the whole personality. New qualities of mind and character are called forth out of ordinary men and women, qualities which manifest the divine in them.

There is a power that seizes

> ". . . such seething brains,
> Such shaping fantasies, that apprehend
> More than cool reason ever comprehends."
> Shakespeare: *Midsummer Night's Dream*, V, 1.

5

Spiritual Life and Living Faiths

ALL religions are founded on the personal experiences of the seers who become directly aware of an Infinite Spiritual Presence beyond and within the range of the world of change and succession. The personal experience of union with Absolute Reality or God has been a common and continuous feature of all the faiths of mankind.

I. HINDUISM

Indian people have been powerfully and continuously affected from ancient times by the idea of religion as direct experience of the Divine. Vidyā, vision, wisdom, is the goal of the Upaniṣads. It is a new kind of thinking in which the whole man, not merely his intellect, is implicated. Experience of the Supreme or *brahmānubhava* is a direct and active participation in the truth, the affirmation of the supreme identity of man in the depths of his being with the Transcendent Reality. This identity is known intuitively in the highest reaches of consciousness. This experience is self-authenticating.

The Upaniṣads assert the oneness of the inward self and the Transcendent Being. "Now if a man worships another deity, thinking the deity is one thing and he another, he does not know." Again, "He who dwells in all beings, and within all beings, whom all beings do not know, whose body all beings are, he is thy self, the ruler within, the immortal."

If man does not recognise the immortal in him he is subject to the law of karma, of necessity. He becomes a puppet, pulled hither and thither by invisible forces. He does nothing but things happen to him. Man is a complex being. The idea of unity is caused by the organic sensibility or possession of a body, by the name which remains the same whatever changes are produced and by a number of mechanical habits which he acquires by imitation or education. He believes himself to be the same individual because he bears the same name, possesses the same physical sensations, notices the same habits and inclinations. If he recognises the Universal Self in him, he begins to act from a new basis of freedom.

In the *Bhagavadgītā,* contemplation of the Supreme is mixed up with devotion to the Absolute as God. Spiritual realisation or contacting ultimate reality, *brahmasaṁsparśa* or communion with the Supreme, *kṛṣṇārjunasaṁvāda* is the goal. The soul, being a portion of the Lord or a fragment of the divine,[1] what the Western mystics call an "uncreated spark" of the divine, returns to its home in God. The emphasis in the *Bhagavadgītā* is on prayer and devotion. The soul is carried by grace beyond images and concepts and enjoys a foretaste of the final object of its desire.[2]

In Vaiṣṇava developments centring round the worship of Rāma or Kṛṣṇa, we have the realisation of the Supreme through devotion and love. Rāmānanda, and Tulsidās, Cai-

---

[1] XV, 7.

[2] In a verse attributed to Śaṁkara, it is said that devotion to God is the easiest pathway to self-realisation.

      mokṣa-sādhana-sāmagryām bhaktir eva garīyasī

      sva-svarūpānusandhānam bhaktir ity abhidhīyate.

tanya, Tukārām and the Marātha saints, Mīrabāi stress the
desire to get near God through a personal inward experience.
The seeker is compared to a child who has lost his mother.
Tukārām says:

> As a child cries out and is sore distressed,
> When its mother it cannot see,
> As a fish that is taken from out the wave,
> So 'tis, says Tukā, with me;

Māṇikkavāsagar and the Śaiva saints of the South worship the
Supreme as Śiva and wish to draw near to him through bhakti
or devotion.

Kabīr, Nānak and the Sikh teachers belong to the devotional
school. Look at the following saying of Kabīr:

> "I laugh when I hear that the fish in the water is thirsty.
> You wander restlessly from forest to forest while the Reality
> is within your own dwelling. . . . The truth is here! Go
> where you will—to Banaras or to Mathura; until you have
> found God in your own soul, the whole world will seem
> meaningless to you."

He tells the seeker: "Your Lord is near; yet you are climbing
the palm-tree to seek him."

Rāmakṛṣṇa, Devendranāth Tagore, Ramaṇa Maharṣi are
among our modern spiritual seers.

The aim of Hindu religion is regeneration of mankind, a
spiritual mutation of human nature. Religion is essentially rebirth, *dvitiyaṁ janma*. This rebornness relates to the inward
man. It is to become new, reach a higher level of understanding. Man belongs to the two levels of time and eternity. The
distinction between the two is qualitative. A quantitative extension of time cannot produce eternity. *Nāsty akṛtaḥ kṛtena,*

as the Upaniṣad says. No amount of temporal experience can give us a glimpse into eternity. Our thought must be lifted to another order of reality above time.

The *Yoga Sūtra* gives a detailed account of the place of prayer, abstraction and contemplation in the pattern of spiritual life.

Throughout the history of Indian religions, Hinduism and Buddhism, Jainism and Sikhism, Christianity and Islam, the stress is more on the renewal of life, the attainment of the transcendental consciousness, than on the worship of personal God, important as the latter is in the theistic religions. Even today many religious people aim at attaining the type of consciousness in which the distinctions of subject and object are fused into an undivided state. In the state of ecstasy or transcendental consciousness, the individual soul feels itself invaded by and merged with an enfolding presence, exalted with a sense of having found what it always has sought.

2. TAOISM

Even before Lao-tse (6th century B.C.), the Chinese looked upon Tao as the Absolute Reality, anterior to and higher than heaven, existing before time began and the manifested God arose. It is the eternal, unchanging, all-pervading principle of which all other developments are manifestations. It is the first cause of all existence, manifesting itself in the Creator and the created universe. It is the root of all phenomena, the principle by which all nature is ordered and controlled. Tao is the source from which all things proceed, the goal to which all things tend.

No name is adequate to describe the principle. It is the Way, Tao. We can speak of it in negative terms, colourless, soundless, immaterial. Out of Tao comes the One, the Great Monad, the material cause of the universe. The One produces the two primary essences, the *Yang* and the *Yin,* the male and the female, light and shade, which give birth to heaven, earth and man, whose interaction results in the production of all creatures.

Tao is in man though it is generally unmanifested. If we are to regain our tranquillity, we should set out on the quest of Tao.

The Chinese book *Tao Teh Ching* teaches the importance of attaining that vacuity and extinction of desire which alone can induce the possession of Tao. Lao-tse says "Only one who is eternally free from earthly passions can apprehend the spiritual essence of Tao." Absolute self-abnegation is the prerequisite for it. We should avoid all preconceptions, lay aside intellectual consciousness, throw open every avenue of thought and feeling to the entrance of Tao. This stage is what is called purgation.

The goal of Taoist ambition is to attain unity with Tao, when one becomes the unresisting vehicle of Tao, free from the limitations imposed by the laws of the world on those who have not reached this state. When unity is attained, we regain tranquillity. Tse Hsia says: "The man who achieves harmony with *Tao* enters into close unison with external objects, and none of them has the power to harm or hinder him."

Real virtue is the spontaneous expression of the Tao within and not an artificial conformity to moral commands. Only when the root Tao is present, the flowers, the virtues, bloom spontaneously.

The Tao is potentially available to all and so each one has to treat others with sympathy. "To the good I would be good, to the not-good I would also be good, in order to make them good."

In Zen Buddhism, dhyāna or meditation is insisted on. We have had a succession of mystics in the Taoist and the Buddhist religions in China.

3. JUDAISM

For the Hebrews, the voice of God is heard in the prophetic consciousness. Scriptural sayings become living truths in personal experience. Moses communing with God in the mountain, Elijah in the cave are instances. In the third Chapter of the Book of Exodus, we are told that the Lord or the angel of the Lord appeared to Moses "in a flame of fire out of the midst of a bush; and he looked, and beheld the bush burned with fire, and the bush was not consumed. And Moses said, I will now turn aside and see this great sight, why the bush is not burnt. And the Lord . . . called unto him out of the midst of the bush and said . . . Draw not nigh hither; put off thy shoes from off thy feet, for the place whereon thou standest is holy ground. . . . And Moses hid his face, for he was afraid to look upon God." Isaiah's vision of God whose "train filled the Temple" points to the all inclusiveness of the Supreme, reminding us of the *viśvarūpa* of the *Bhagavadgītā*.[3] The universe is one uninterrupted revelation of the Divine. The insatiable craving of the human spirit for the Divine comes out in the Psalmist's utterance: "Whom have I in heaven but thee? And there is none upon earth whom I desire but thee." [4] "Yea, I have loved thee with an everlasting love; therefore with loving kindness have I drawn thee." [5]

[3] XI.
[4] Psalm 73:25.
[5] Jeremiah 31:3.

When the theology of Judaism was studied along with the works of Plato and Aristotle, a curious blend of Jewish and Greek thought arose of which the chief works are the writings of Philo, the Wisdom of Solomon and the fragments of Aristobulus preserved by Eusebius. Aristobulus upholds the Jewish doctrine of God that he is at once transcendent and immanent. He is greater than the world and separate from it and yet he works in the universe by means of his "wisdom," which is an emanation from him and yet has no separate existence from him. God is in his heaven and yet "the earth is his footstool."

If holy God cannot come into relations with impure men, his angels can. Angels are the emanations of God, offshoots of deity. Wisdom is represented as the Logos, "for she is the breath of the power of God, and a pure influence flowing from the glory of the Almighty; therefore can no defiled thing fall into her. For she is the brightness of the everlasting light, the unspotted mirror of the power of God, and the image of his goodness. And being but one, she can do all things; and remaining in herself, she maketh all things new; and in all ages entering into holy souls, she maketh them friends of God, and prophets. For God loveth none but him that dwelleth with wisdom." [6] "To be attuned into wisdom is immortality." [7]

Philo makes a sharp distinction between God in himself and God revealed. God in himself is Pure Being, unknowable, transcendent, outside the universe; God revealed is immanent in man and the universe, all-pervading, all-filling. Through his angels, God intervenes in the world. For Philo, the universe is filled with divine potencies. They are in one sense revelations

[6] Wisdom of Solomon, 7:25 ff.
[7] *Ibid.*, 8:17.

of God and in another personal beings of a spiritual kind, incorporeal souls. There are various gradations among these potencies and at the head of them is the Logos, which constitutes the principle of unity. Heaven and earth subsisted in the Logos before their material creation. God works through the Logos who works through the potencies called *Logoi*.

Rabbinic mysticism found its expression in the mediaeval Kabbālā, whose most famous manual is *Zohār*. According to it, the world is an embodiment of God, who is a being utterly devoid of attributes and can only be described negatively. The world comes into contact with God only through intermediaries, which are the ten emanations. The first manifestation is a unity which is unanalysable, and yet possesses all. It is the primordial divine thought or will, which, emanating from God, contains within itself the plan of the universe with its infinite extent and endless variety. Wisdom and Intelligence are the second and the third emanations. There is a relationship between them. Wisdom is the father, the masculine, active principle which engenders all things and imposes form and measure on them. Intelligence is the mother, the passive receptive principle. From their union comes the son who is reason, who reflects the characteristics of both.[8] The remaining seven principles are mercy, justice, beauty, victory, glory, foundation and royalty. The *Zohār* emphasises the deep spirituality of prayer and its capacity to bring about changes in the material world. Maimonides, the chief exponent of the mediaeval Jewish scholasticism, insists on the *via negativa* and Spinoza's *Ethics* is of profound importance to religious life.

[8] These three answer to puruṣa, prakṛti and mahat or buddhi of the Sāṁkhya philosophy.

4. GREEK RELIGION

There are two currents of thought in the ancient Greek religion, the Homeric and the Mystic. In the Eleusinian faith the highest initiate is a beholder. He is shown things and is convinced of his salvation by the evidence of his own eyes. The initiate does not learn anything but undergoes an experience, after suitable preparation. There is no doctrine in connection with Eleusis. The poet Sophocles and the painter Polygnotus confine happiness in the next world to those who had been initiated into the mysteries of Eleusis. Cicero expresses the view that Athens had produced nothing better than the mysteries of Eleusis both in regard to the ordering and civilising of life and the furnishing of a good hope in death.[9]

Dionysiac mysteries, which were marked by wild ecstasy and several barbaric rites, take on an important aspect when associated with the name of Orpheus. The Orphic societies were generally attached to the worship of Dionysus, though sometimes other deities took his place. Those who were eager for communion with the Divine and anxious to attain peace of mind and a position of hope and confidence amid the blows of circumstances were attracted to the mystery religions.

In Plato and Plotinus the two currents coalesce. For Plato, the end of life is "to become like God." True piety is to be a fellow worker with God.[10] In the Pauline Epistles and the Fourth Gospel we find the influence of the mystery religions in the rites of initiation and of communion. Many of the intellectual elements of the Orphic and the Eleusinian mysteries were taken over by the gnostic sects.

Plotinus (A.D. 205–270) makes out that his doctrine is not

[9] *De Legibus*, ii, 14.
[10] *Euthyphro*.

anything new. "This doctrine is not new; it was professed from the most ancient times, though without being developed explicitly; we wish only to be interpreters of the ancient sages, and to show by the evidence of Plato himself that they had the same opinions as ourselves." [11] Plotinus had on four occasions the experience of God according to Porphyry during his association with him. His friend, the physician Eustochius, heard his last words: "I was waiting for you, before the divine principle in me departs to unite itself with the divine in the universe."

The Supreme is beyond existence, beyond life. It abides in a state of wakefulness beyond being.[12] We cannot call it good; it is perfection. It is beauty, not the beautiful.[13] Plotinus distinguishes between Godhead and God. The God whom we worship is the revelation, not the revealer. The source of revelation cannot be revealed. The goal of the intellect is the One; the goal of will is goodness; the goal of love and admiration is beauty. As W. R. Inge says: "The Absolute *must be*—that is the conclusion of the dialectic; it *ought to be*—this is the conclusion of ethics; it *is*—this is the discovery of the spirit in love." [14] We can know the Absolute because we are ourselves, in our deepest ground, the Absolute. We see the Ultimate Spirit "not through the discursive reason, but by some spiritual contact, about which we may reason afterwards, but not at the time. We must believe that the soul has truly seen, when it suddenly perceives a light. We must believe that God is present, when he comes into the house of him who invites him and

[11] *Enneads*, V, 1, 8.
[12] *Enneads*, V, 3–13. VIII, 17.
[13] *Ibid.*, VI, 7, 8.
[14] Article on "Neo-Platonism," *Encyclopaedia of Religion and Ethics,* Vol. IX, p. 315.

gives him life. . . . This is the soul's true goal, to touch that light, and to behold it by means of that light itself, and not by any other light; even as we see not the sun by any light except its own." [15] This ecstatic state is a rare phenomenon gained only at the summit of spiritual development. Porphyry, Iamblichus, Proclus developed Neo-Platonism after Plotinus.

5. ZOROASTRIANISM

Though the number of Zoroastrians is small, the thought embodied in the Gāthas of Zarathustra is profound and universal in its significance. Zarathustra himself, it is said, was born in response to the appeal of Mother Earth to help mankind to overcome evil. Ahura-Mazdā says that he was "the only one who kept all our commands." When Zarathustra was meditating on the laws of Ahura-Mazdā, it is said, the Evil One Angrō-Mainyu tempted him with the sovereignty of the world if only he would renounce his faith in Ahura-Mazdā. He chanted the famous verse *Ahura-Vairya* and the wicked one fled. This story refers to a spiritual crisis through which Zarathustra passed when he made his choice for the pursuit of truth and right against falsehood and wrong. The dualism is within one's own nature. The evil forces are within man and not outside. When it is said that man is possessed by evil spirits, it means that he is under the power of evil impulses and thoughts. His growth is prevented because he consents to these forces. The evil powers, self-love, malice, vanity, ignorance in mistaking the outer appearances for the only reality, are collectively called the Devil or the Evil One. That Zarathustra overcame the Evil One means that he did not succumb to these forces. His conduct demonstrates that man's own self

[15]*Enneads,* V, 3, 17.

determines his destiny. The Evil One who is called Satan in the latest books of the Old Testament is remarkably similar to Angrō-Mainyu of the later Avesta.

Ahura-Mazdā is the Supreme Being, the Lord of life and matter, the cosmic Lord Īśvara from whom have sprung puruṣa and prakṛti. There are six Holy Immortals, associated with the three rays of the Father side and three of the Mother side. These are aspects or emanations of the Supreme. *Asha* is the first ray, representing the will of God which planned out the universe. It stands for truth and righteousness. The second is *Vohu-mano* who symbolises the love of the Supreme. The third is *Kṣattra,* who represents the creative activity of the Supreme. The fourth *Ārmaiti* typifies the Mother side of the Supreme, love and understanding. She is the indwelling spirit. *Haurvatāt* is the ideal which every human being has, the principle of spiritual growth. The last, *Ameratatāt,* is the principle of immortality, of strength. These six are not entities or abstractions but an integral part of God's being.

Zarathustra declares that the union with the Supreme is the highest ideal and the way to it is through *asha* by which we gain purity of mind, heart and soul. Through *asha* "may we get a vision of Thee, may we draw near unto Thee, may we be in perfect union with Thee." "There is but one path—the path of *Asha*—all others are false paths." (*Yasna,* 60, 12; 71, 11.)

The Avestan *asha* and the Vedic *ṛta* are two variants of the same word and the underlying thought was fully developed in the period before the Indian Āryans and the Iranians separated. The highest principle Ahura-Mazdā acts according to changeless laws which express his mind. The cosmic process is progressing towards its fulfilment according to the law of *asha.*

They are the saints who understand the supreme wisdom of
asha and act in its spirit. Only those acts done out of love for
the Supreme give us happiness and not those which are performed for one's own good. Unselfish work is the way by
which human individuals attain their spiritual welfare and
help the progress of the world.

Love in Zoroastrian religion embraces the animal world
also. On four days (2, 12, 14, 21) in every month, orthodox
Zoroastrians abstain from meat-eating. A few eat no meat during the whole of the eleventh month of the year.

Zarathustra promises those who follow his teaching everlasting life. It is a mystery which he offers to those who seek to
know. The dualism between good and evil continues till the
end of the cosmic process, when the forces of evil are completely broken. The omnipotence of the right is established for
ever. Zarathustra is convinced that the world will be regen-
erated and redeemed. To know the Supreme Ahura-Mazdā
and act according to his law *asha*, one has to perfect one's
nature through prayer and meditation. When we reach the
goal we realise peace and unity.

6. BUDDHISM

The Buddha does not profess to teach a new way. "I have
seen the ancient way, the old road that was taken by the
former awakened beings and that is the path I follow." [16] The
Buddha speaks of bodhi or enlightenment. It is an immediate,
non-discursive, intuitive relation with Absolute Truth. It is
not theoretical knowledge. It is knowledge that cuts the roots
of desire and is the result of concentration on the nature of
Being. It is a correct act of attention, *yoniśo manasikāra*.

[16] *Samyutta Nikāya*, II, 106.

The self is not to be found in the world of becoming. Everything which is an object of knowledge is *anattā,* not-self, but there is a state remote from the objective, released from the influences of *tanha* or craving, beyond sorrow, beyond suffering.[17] We cannot get to essential Being through the outer trappings.[18] Man in the ignorant state forgets his real nature and identifies himself with what he is not. He must get to know the truth beyond all phenomenal existence. "Be such as have the self (ātman) as your lamp, the self as the only refuge; the law as the lamp and the only refuge." [19]

Prajñā is not a state of illumination with no object to illuminate, not a mirror that reflects nothing. It is a consciousness that transcends subject-object distinctions, what the *Māṇḍūkya Upaniṣad* calls turīya or transcendental consciousness. It is a state of freedom from contingency. The Buddhist texts often refer to an unborn (ajāta), an uncaused, an immutable, and the way leading to it. The path to Nirvāṇa is the ethical path. The Buddha in the spirit of the Upaniṣads protests against mere ritualism and insists on inward discipline. "If the mere wearing of the robe could banish greed, malice, etc., then as soon as a child was born, his friends and kinsfolk would make him wear the robe, and would press him to wear it, saying 'come, thou favoured of fortune! come, wear the robe,' for by the mere wearing of it, the greedy will put away from them their greed and the malicious their malice." [20]

In the spirit of the Upaniṣads, the Buddha asks us to free ourselves from the dominion of time. We can do so by freeing ourselves from desire. If we refuse to feed the flame of *tanha*

[17] aśokam virajam padam. *Itivuttaka,* 51.
[18] na so upādhisu sāram eti. *Suttanipāta,* 364.
[19] Dīgha Nikāya, II, 101.
[20] *Further Dialogues of the Buddha* (1926), Part I, p. 200.

or craving, the fire would go out for want of fuel. Nirvāna is liberation from resentment, covetousness, lust. It is not annihilation. It is a state of bliss, ageless, stable, lasting. The Buddha emphasises the sense of freedom and spontaneity, clarity of vision, and tranquil joy.

Buddha's refusal to speculate on the nature of Nirvāna does not mean that it is nothing but that it is above definition. Adopting the method of reason, the Buddha declined to answer certain ontological questions which he considered to be useless. He rejected the principle of authority, for truths accepted on authority and not ascertained and realised by personal effort are of no avail.

In Mahāyāna Buddhism, the relation of the devotee to the Absolute is mediated by faith and prayer and the devotee is helped by the grace and guidance of the Divine Buddha. In all types of Buddhism, methods of concentration of thought are emphasised.

7. CHRISTIANITY

Jesus' personal experience is a supreme example of direct knowledge. His acts and utterances are penetrated with a feeling of fellowship with God. "The altered fashion of countenance," the transfigured form and face which marked his experience before his journey to Jerusalem indicate a profound spiritual change. When Jesus says about St. John the Baptist that though he is the greatest among men, the least among the blessed in heaven is greater than the greatest man on earth, he means that he who has seen the Truth is greater than he who argues about it and who has not the direct inward knowledge. We must transcend the intellectual point of view and feel the inward, supra-social, spiritual realities.

Jesus demands an inward renewal, an inner change. The

Kingdom of Heaven is not a place in space but a state of mind. The Kingdom is present, here, immediate. "Repent, for the Kingdom of Heaven is at hand." It is the attainment of Truth which makes for freedom or liberation. Jesus refers to the inner perfecting, the possible evolution of man. When he asks us to "repent," he means not penitence or regret but an inward revolution. The Greek word of which repentance is the English translation is *meta-noia*, the raising of one's consciousness beyond its normal dimensions. It is the change of the inner man. When Jesus says, "Except ye turn and become as little children," [21] he means that we should wake up from the world of objects, from the sleep of the senses. The dead man must become alive again. We must come back to ourselves, liberated from our jealousies and hatreds. "Unless ye repent, ye cannot enter the Kingdom of Heaven." We must attain to a higher level of being through violence to our own lower nature, through abstinence and self-control.

"Ye must be born again from above." It is not the natural, physical birth but a spiritual rebirth. A proper reconditioning of man's whole nature is the meaning of salvation. The law is spiritual. St. Paul writes: "So then with the mind I myself serve the Law of God, but with the flesh the law of sin." "For I delight in the law of God after the inward man." [22]

He who is liberated is lifted above the law. "The Sabbath is made for man, not man for the Sabbath." [23] Love is the fulfilment of law.

The religious secret, *rahasya* or mystery is transmitted from teacher to pupil. Jesus had this spiritual wisdom, which he did not wish to teach to all and sundry without discrimination.

[21] Matthew 18:3.
[22] Romans 7:25, 22.
[23] Mark 2:27.

"Give not that which is Holy unto the dogs, neither cast ye
your pearls before swine, lest they trample them under their
feet, and turn again and rend you." [24]

True religion is the remaking of the soul by contemplative
prayer and ascetic practice. Jesus' thirty years of silence and
forty days of silence in the desert are the preparation for his
spiritual attainment. Jesus was the son of man and the son of
God. He had contact with both levels, the earthly and the
heavenly. As a human being he was exposed to every temptation. Up to the last moment he was tempted. "My God, why
hast thou forsaken me?" He suffered agony. Jesus was an example to men for he raised himself through battling with inner
discords, doubts and temptations. In climbing the ladder of
inner development he had to suffer a great deal.

The incarnation is not an historical event which occurred
two thousand years ago. It is an event which is renewed in the
life of everyone who is on the way to the fulfilment of his
destiny. Meister Eckhart refers to the aim of religion as the
birth of God in the soul of man. "The supreme purpose of
God is birth. He will not be content until his son is born in us.
Neither will the soul be content until the son is born of it." [25]
Birth here means God-manifestation, God-realisation.

When it is said that the Son of Man will come again, it

[24] In his work on the Holy Ghost, St. Basil speaks of a "tacit and
mystical tradition maintained down to our own times, and of a secret instruction that our fathers observed without discussion and which we
follow by dwelling in the simplicity of their silence. For they understood
how necessary was silence in order to maintain the respect and veneration
due to our Holy Mysteries. And in fact it was not expedient to make
known in writing a doctrine containing things that catechumens are not
permitted to contemplate." According to St. Denys the Areopagite, "salvation is possible only for deified souls, and deification is nothing else
but the union and resemblance we strive to have with God."
[25] *Sermon* 12.

means that when truth wears itself out, when the world loses its contact with the higher level of spirit, when it is bogged down in violence and materiality, then Truth will have to appear in a new form. The same transcendent Truth is given in different forms with slight changes of emphasis to suit different conditions. When a period of chaos arises, when righteousness languishes, the Spirit of Truth will come down again. Each manifestation is a second coming of the Son of Man, of the divine being taking on the garb of humanity, raising himself up through the overcoming of human temptations, re-establishing order and opening the way to human development. These manifestations, incarnations, avatāras further the purpose of man to pass from a lower to a higher level of understanding.

St. Paul has direct knowledge of God in view when he says: "For now we see in a mirror darkly but then face to face." In many passages, St. Paul describes the experience of Divine Presence.[26] He had a vivid consciousness of the interrelation of the human spirit and the Divine. "To live is Christ." We partake of the divine nature. We are saved if we renew our being and relive a life which reveals God. St. Paul's whole teaching was based on an immediate, divine, environing presence in whom we live, move and have our being. St. Paul asks Christians to effect a change in their minds. "Let the mind be in you which was also in Christ Jesus." "If any man be in Christ, there is a new creation, behold, all things are become new." St. Paul spent three years before his apostolate in the desert. We find references to visions and dreams, to gifts of the Holy Ghost in St. Paul and other Christian works.

[26] Galatians 1:15, 16; 2:20; 4:6; II Corinthians 3:18; 4:6; 12:1-4; Romans 8:2, 16; Ephesians 3:14-21.

K

There are indications of the influence of the Eastern mystery religions which were invading the Roman Empire in St. Paul's time. He makes a distinction between his usual preaching about "Jesus Christ and him crucified," and a divine wisdom which God decreed before the ages for our glorification, a wisdom that is hidden and intended only for the mature, a wisdom that reveals to us "what no eye hath seen nor ear heard, nor the heart of man conceived." [27] The servants of Christ are, for St. Paul, "stewards of the mysteries of God." [28]

St. John is greatly influenced by Plato. There are for him two worlds, the true and real world that is above and the world of darkness and shadow. Jesus is eternally of God and in him is life of the real and eternal order. Jesus reveals to us in this world the nature of the world of spirit and the light of God. For John, Christ is the Wisdom of God immanent in the cosmos. The work of Christ is of cosmic significance. The Logos doctrine affirms that the whole universe is reaching its maturity and returning to perfection through Christ.[29] "He is the image of the invisible God, the first born of all creation . . . all things were created through him and for him." [30] The world process is one of conflict and victory. The victory over the hostile forces is a cosmic victory and this victory brings about a new relation, a relation of reconciliation between God and the world.

The Alexandrian theologians, Clement (A.D. 215) and Origen (A.D. 251) did not hesitate to describe Christianity itself as a "mystery religion" or as "the true gnosticism" though they

[27] I Corinthians 2:9.
[28] I Corinthians 4:1.
[29] Cf. *Taittirīya Upaniṣad* III.
[30] Colossians 1:15–16.

were later condemned as heretics.[31] From Philo, Clement borrowed the idea that God is to be sought in the darkness.[32] He is to be reached by faith and abstraction. "Going forth by analysis to the First Intelligence, (taking away depth, breadth, length and position, leaving a monad, then abstracting what is material) if we cast ourselves into the vastness of Christ, thence if we proceed forward by holiness into his immensity, we may in some fashion enter into the knowledge of the Almighty recognising not what he is, but what he is not." [33]

Origen refers frequently to contemplation and speaks of rising above sense and mind to the one unspeakable vision. He lived an austere life and claimed that one could attain communion with God and spiritual gifts by abstinence and discipline.

With the development of monachism in the fourth century, prayer without images and contemplation were exalted. The founder of Egyptian monachism, St. Anthony, sometimes remained all night in ecstasy. "And he also delivered this celestial and more than human judgment as to the end of prayer. 'That prayer is not perfect in which the man understands himself or his own prayer.' " [34]

St. Augustine's saying, "Thou hast created us for thyself and our heart is restless till it finds its rest in thee," is well known. The core of his religion is derived from his personal experience, direct relation between the human soul and God. He often refers to mystical insight. "Lo, now we have rejoiced in

[31] See E. C. Dewick: *The Christian Attitude to Other Religions* (1953), p. 121.
[32] *Stromata* I, 2; V, 12.
[33] *Ibid.*, V, 11.
[34] Cassian, *Collation,* IX, 31.

some inward sweetness; lo, in the summit of the mind we have been able to see something that is unchangeable, in a momentary flash." [35]

We had a number of contemplatives in the Thebaid in the fourth century. After the fall of Rome, Christianity flourished owing to the withdrawal of St. Benedict (A.D. 543) and the schooling which thousands of his disciples had in prayer and work. St. Benedict insists on the condition for contemplative prayer, separation from the world, obedience, silence, humility which will lead the monk to perfect charity. [36]

Pseudo-Dionysius (end of the fifth century) and St. Gregory the Great (end of the sixth century) had great influence on the Middle Ages. In his *Mystical Theology,* Pseudo-Dionysius distinguishes the philosophical from the mystical approach. The philosophical gives us an abstract idea; the mystical carries the soul above intelligence into union. The mystical ascent is described as the entry into the "super-lucent darkness of hidden mystic silence." [37]

Throughout the Middle Ages the advice given by Pseudo-Dionysius on the practice of contemplation was used: "And thou, dear Timothy, in thy intent practice of the mystical contemplations, leave behind both thy senses and thy intellectual operations, and all things known by senses and intellect and all things which are not and which are, and set thyself as far as may be, to unite thyself in unknowing with him who is above all being and knowledge, for by being purely free and absolute, out of self and of all things, thou shalt be led up to the ray of the divine darkness, stripped of all, and loosed from all."

[35] On Psalm 41:10.
[36] *Reg.,* 7.
[37] *Mystical Theology,* I.

St. Gregory the Great is greatly influenced by Augustine. For him the contemplative life is higher than the active. Jesus' life is an example of the union of the two lives where the active does not impede the tranquillity of mind. The conditions for the contemplative life include tranquillity and retirement, severe self-discipline and love of God and of the neighbour.

St. Bernard of Clairvaux (twelfth century) had great influence on the history of spiritual religion. "I confess," he says, "that the Word has visited me and even very often. But although He has frequently entered into my soul, I have never at any time been sensible of His coming. I have felt that He was present; I remember that He has been with me; I have sometimes been able even to have a presentiment that He would come; but never to feel His coming or His departure." After relating that God does not enter through the senses, he says: "He is living and full of energy, and as soon as He has entered into me, He has quickened my sleeping soul, has aroused and softened and goaded my heart, which was in a state of torpor and hard as a stone." [38]

Richard of St. Victor (1173) distinguishes between the philosophical approach through discussion and reasoning and the contemplative attitude when the mind goes forth out of itself and sees the truth without any veil.

The thirteenth century saw a great wave of spiritual religion. The Franciscan, St. Bonaventura (1274) says: "I admit, however, that the mind's eye can be fixed on God in such wise that it looks at naught else; yet it will not perceive nor see the glory of the Light itself, but will rather be raised up into the darkness; and to this knowledge it will be elevated by the removal of all things as Dionysius says, and he calls this knowledge

[38] *Sermon on the Mount,* Canticle LXXIV, 5, 6, 7.

'learned ignorance.' For this knowledge it is in which the affection is set on fire, as is well known to those who are accustomed to ecstasy. In my opinion this manner of knowledge is to be sought by every just man in this life." [39] "If you ask how this takes place, inquire of grace, not of learning, of desire, not of intelligence, of the groaning of prayer, not of the study of understanding." [40]

The Dominican Albertus Magnus (1280) insists on internal recollection, the stripping of the mind naked of all phantasms and images when it becomes tranquillised in God. St. Thomas Aquinas (1274) believes in the beatific vision of God as he is, in which God is seen by means of himself. He is both the thing seen and the means by which it is seen. The blessed participate in the act in which God knows himself without medium and are united to him as Act for God is *actus purus,* insofar as may be without ceasing to be themselves.

In the beginning of the Fourth book of *Summa Contra Gentiles,* St. Thomas Aquinas speaks of three kinds of human knowledge of divine things: "The first of these is the knowledge that comes by the natural light of reason," when the reason ascends by means of creatures to God. The second "descends to us by way of revelation." The third is possible only to the human mind "elevated to the perfect intuition of the things that are revealed." Following St. Augustine, Thomas Aquinas admitted that the beatific vision was granted to Moses and to St. Paul. This vision is the end for which man is made and this is his reward. St. Thomas Aquinas himself had a direct experience of the Divine and told his disciple Reginald

[39] *Comm. in Sent.* II, dist. 23, art. 2, Qu3 concl.
[40] *Itinerarium.*

that all that he had written was utterly futile compared to the riches of the vision of God.

Joachim of Floria in the twelfth century sees the story of man in three stages, the first is of the Father, of the letter of the Law, where we have to listen and obey. The second is of the Son; we have here argument and criticism. Tradition is explained; authority is explicated. The third stage is of the spirit, where we have prayer and song, meditation and inspiration.[41]

In Dante (1265–1321) we find the most complete expression of the mediaeval world. The *Divine Comedy* is a pilgrim's progress. It is called a comedy because it has a happy ending but the path to freedom leads through the underworld of sin and expiation. In the journey to God, there are three stages by which the advance is made: (1) The natural light of reason which operates through that stretch of the way where Vergil is guide, from the door of Hell up to the summit of Purgatory; (2) the light of grace which, in the figure of Beatrice as guide, presides on the upward way from the summit of Purgatory to that other summit in Paradise where she leaves Dante to take her seat in the great rose of heaven; and (3) that light of glory which begins to descend and to be accessible to the wayfarer following upon the prayer by St. Bernard, making possible the final upward advance to the ultimate vision.

We have had other great mystics, St. Hildegard (1179), the two Mechtildes (13th century), Angela of Foligno (1309), Julian of Norwich (1412), whose writings had profound influence on spiritual life. St. Catherine of Siena (fourteenth century) at the tender age of six was suddenly inspired by a heavenly vision of the Saviour of the world. This experience

---

[41] See Gerald Heard, *The Eternal Gospel* (1948), p. 6.

affected her whole subsequent life and led her into paths of ecstasy and mortification.

In England, we have had mystics, Margerie Kempe (1290), Richard Rolle of Hampole (1349), Walter Hilton (1396), a Carthusian who was much influenced by Rolle and whose work *The Scale of Perfection* is well known, and the unknown author of *The Cloud of Unknowing*, an excellent guide for contemplative prayer.

In Germany, Meister Eckhart (1327) who submitted to censure with all humility,[42] Henry Suso (1366) of an austere poetical temperament, Tauler (1361), the great preacher, and his follower Ruysbroeck are well known. *Theologia Germanica* appeared about 1350 and exercised profound influence on religious life. This, and Thomas a Kempis' *The Imitation of Christ* were the great classics of mediaeval mysticism. Luther studied *Theologia Germanica* and Tauler's *Sermons* and his accounts of religious experience indicate that spiritual insight into the meaning of faith is the way to personal salvation. Paracelsus, who died in 1545, had direct experience of the Universal Life suffused throughout nature. For him, man is an integral part of this life.

Jacob Boehme (1575–1624) tells us that thrice in his life he was immersed in a condition of ecstasy which lasted for days during which he felt himself surrounded by a divine light. On the second occasion nature lay unveiled to him and he was at home in the heart of things. Of his third experience Boehme wrote: "The gate was opened to me, that in one quarter of

---

[42] "In Eckhart the Dionysian current, reinforced by further neo-Platonic elements derived from Proclus and the Arabs, reaches its extreme development and seems to pass the utmost bounds of orthodoxy and to bring the mediaeval theological development to a conclusion not far removed from the pure monism of the Vedānta." Christopher Dawson, *Mediaeval Essays* (1953), p. 108.

an hour I saw and knew more than if I had been many years together at an University." What Boehme calls the *Ungrund, Mysterium Magnum,* the Abyss of Freedom, is the basis of all existence, which is beyond the categories of time and space. This is the primaeval stillness. We need the opposites, and their tension for manifestation.

After Pascal's death there was found stitched into the lining of his doublet a scrap of parchment with a rough drawing of a flaming cross and a few words around it to keep alive the memory of his experience:

> In the year of grace 1654, Monday, 23rd November, the day of St. Clement, Pope and Martyr, and others in the Martyrology;
> The eve of St. Chrysogonus, Martyr and others, from about half past ten in the evening till about half an hour after midnight.

> Fire

> God of Abraham, God of Isaac, God of Jacob. Not of the philosophers and of the learned.
> Certitude. Joy. Certitude. Emotion. Sight. Joy.
> Forgetfulness of the world and of all outside of God.
> The world hath not known Thee, but I have known Thee.
> Joy! Joy! Joy! Tears of Joy.
> My God, wilt Thou leave me?
> Let me not be separated from Thee for ever.[43]

George Fox (1624–1691) came under the influence of Boehme and he went through a spiritual experience which gave him remarkable insight and power. There is "light" or "seed" of God in every man. When the soul triumphs over the tendencies to evil and is obedient to the divine endowment, it

[43] Dom Cuthbert Butler, *Western Mysticism* (1922), p. 15.

becomes an instrument or organ of the Inward Light. Through silent worship and suppression of selfishness we receive divine grace and become sanctified.

William Law (1686–1761) was greatly influenced by Boehme and the English Platonists, Whichcote, Smith, More and Cudworth. His writings disclose his religious insight and consciousness of direct inward relation to Invisible Reality.

English poets of the seventeenth century, John Donne, George Herbert, Thomas Traherne, Henry Vaughan, were strongly influenced by classical mysticism. William Blake (1757–1827) was of a marked psychical disposition and his writings were distinctly mystical as Emerson's were in America. In the nineteenth century, Wordsworth, Coleridge, Tennyson and Browning revealed in their writings their own personal experience and insight into the soul's deepest life.

Jean Gerson (1429) wrote a work on *Mystica Theologia* which places the mystic faculty in what he calls the *apex mentis*. Nicholas of Cusa (1464), who bases his views on neo-Platonism, and the Benedictine Blosius (1565) support the practice of prayer leading to "union with God without any medium."

The two great writers on mysticism of the sixteenth century come from Spain, St. Theresa (1582) and St. John of the Cross (1591). St. Theresa gives us vivid descriptions of the inner experience of a saint. She distinguishes the degrees of prayer according to their psychological effects. In her earliest work, *Life,* she distinguishes meditation, in which the powers of the soul act naturally and freely; recollection, or prayer of quiet in which the will is united to God while the imagination and intellect remain free to help or hinder the union; total dedication, in which all these powers are drawn into union, a complete union of all the powers, which lasts a bare half hour accompanied by rapture and ecstasy. In *The Spiritual Castle,* the spiritual marriage is represented as the goal of the quest.

St. John of the Cross, who is a disciple of St. Theresa, teaches that ecstasy and rapture are due to bodily weakness. In the *Ascent of Mount Carmel,* he treats of the ascetic side of the contemplative life. He demands an utter renunciation and self-abandonment. What he calls the "night of the senses" weans the soul away from sensible devotion and causes a desire for solitude and repose. In this state the soul abandons itself to God without attempting to possess any specific knowledge. After the "night of the senses," we have the night of the spirit in which God humbles, chastens and purifies the higher part of the soul, and prepares it for the perfect union of which St. John of the Cross speaks in his *The Spiritual Canticle* and *The Living Flame of Love.*

St. Francis of Sales (1622) gives a good account of contemplative prayer. Molinos (1696) and Madame Guyon (1717) were led into dangerous extravagances about quietism and contemplatives and mystics became confused with imaginative, feeble-minded, sickly persons.

John Woolman, the travelling Quaker, in his *Diary,* writes: "There is a principle, which is pure, placed in the human mind, which in different places and ages hath had different names; it is, however, pure and proceeds from God. It is deep and inward, confined to no forms of religion, nor excluded from any, where the heart stands in perfect sincerity. In whomsoever this takes root, and grows, of what nation soever, they become brethren."

The religious spirit of the Russian people is of a mystical character and the type of worship that has developed in the

Russian churches fosters mystic feelings. The aim of religion is
to apprehend God in feeling as the all-embracing unity.

Muhammad's mystical nature was repelled by the polytheism
of his compatriots. He devoted himself to retreats and evolved
his reformist religious views.

8. ISLAM: SUFISM

The central feature of Islam is the worship of God and ac-
knowledgment of him as the Absolute Lord. The unity of God
to which the Quran is a glorious testimony seems to Muhammad to be compromised by the Christians, who believe in
martyrs, saints and angels. The mysteries of the Trinity and the
Incarnation contradict divine unity. In their obvious sense,
Eastern Christians introduced three equal deities and transformed Jesus into the substance of the Son of God. Muhammad rejected the worship of men and idols, of stars and
planets, on the principle that whatever rises must set, whatever is born must die, whatever is corruptible must decay and
perish. For Muhammad, God is an Infinite and Eternal Being
without form or place, without issue or similitude. He is present in our most secret thoughts, exists necessarily of his own
nature, and derives from himself all moral and intellectual per-
fections. God is what remains when we abstract from the unknown substance all ideas of time and space, of motion and
matter, of sense and thought. Muhammad and his followers
are unitarians. They complain that the unitarian spirit of the
Christian Gospels is lost in the pageantry of the Church.
Muhammad reproaches Christians for taking their priests and
monks as their lords besides God.

Whatever the theologians may say, Muhammad was a seer
in the ancient tradition. The Quran is the book of a seer.

The Sufi tradition which claims Muhammad as its founder lays stress on personal experience of God. The Sufis were solitaries who made their homes in isolated places and depended for their livelihood on the charity of those who came to pay them homage. Sufism believes that there is only one Ultimate Reality in the universe which is unknowable. We must seek knowledge of it through its names and attributes. Pure Being has no name or attribute. Names and attributes are given to it when it descends from its absoluteness into the realm of manifestation.

The Absolute apart from all qualities and relations is called by the Sufi Jīlī, the "darkness" (al-'amā). He develops consciousness by passing through three stages, oneness, he-ness, I-ness. By this process the Absolute Being becomes the subject and object of all thought and reveals itself as divinity with distinctive attributes embracing the whole series of existences. The phenomenal world is the revelation of the Absolute. Ibn al' Arabī says: "God is necessary to us in order that we may exist, while we are necessary to him, in order that he may be manifested to himself."

The human soul is a part of the Absolute, "imprisoned" within the body. It regains its source when it is freed from the flesh. While all existences display some attribute of Absolute Reality, the human being is the microcosm in which all the attributes are united. The Absolute becomes conscious of itself in man. God and man become one in the perfect man, the prophet or saint who is the final cause of creation.

The germs of the Sufi doctrine are found in the Quran "Everything is perishing (hālik) except the face [reality] of Allāh." [44] "Every one on the earth is passing away [fāni] but

[44] XXVIII, 88.

the glorious and honoured face of thy Lord abideth for
ever." [45] "Wheresoever ye turn there is the face of Allāh." [46]
The unique personality of Allāh far above and beyond human
reach became transformed into the one Real Being revealed in
all created beings. He is the true self of man which he finds
by losing his individual consciousness in ecstatic self-abandonment. The definition of *fanā* as a transcendental state and the
way to it by means of the extinction of all passions and desires
remind us of the Buddhist Nirvāṇa and the way to it. The
Sufis sought for the Supreme "within" through contemplation.

Bayazid of Khurasan says:

I went from God to God, until they cried from me in me,
   "O Thou I!"
Verily, I am God, there is no God except me, so
Worship me. Glory to me! How great is my majesty!

One of the greatest of the Sufis, Al Ḥallāj, who was crucified
for his convictions, speaks of the awareness of the experience
of the self. He calls it *tafrid*. We become aware of the self by
withdrawing from everything else. He describes the condition
of the soul when it is separated from delight in the self and
the condition in which God unites the soul to himself. Suffering for him is not a thing to flee from. It is the means by
which the soul is raised to the divine status.

Al Ḥallāj's statement, *ana al-Ḥaqq*, I am the Truth, is an
echo of the Upaniṣad saying, "I am Brahman," *aham brahmāsmi*. These truths were grasped by the Sufis as a result of
personal experience rather than of philosophical reflection. The
influence of neo-Platonism and Hindu and Buddhist thought
may have inclined them to a mystic interpretation of Islam.

[45] IV, 26 ff.
[46] II, 109.

A story is related of the mystic Basra-Rabia that "One day several Sufis met Rabia running and carrying fire in one hand and water in the other. They said to her, 'O Lady of the world to come, where are you going, and what is the meaning of this?" She replied: 'I am going to set fire to paradise and to drown hell with water, so that those two veils should completely vanish from before the eyes of the pilgrims, and so that their end or purpose be known to them, and God's servants see him, without any motive for hope or fear.[47] What would happen if the hope of paradise or the fear of hell did not exist? Alas, no one would want to adore his God or obey him." We must love God for his own sake. Rabia could not even love the prophet, Muhammad, because her love of God absorbed her so entirely that neither love nor hate of any other being remained in her heart.

The Sufis felt that their realisation of religion was compatible with the observance of the law and even included it as one aspect of their realisation. He who comprehends the Divine

[47] Cf. Ibrāhim Adham: "O God, Thou knowest that, in mine eyes, the Eight Paradises weigh no more than the wing of a gnat compared with that honour which Thou hast shown me in giving me Thy love, or that familiarity which Thou hast given to me by the commemoration of Thy Name, or that freedom from all else which Thou hast vouchsafed to me when I meditate on the greatness of Thy Glory."

Attār quotes a saying of Ibrāhim Adham and comments: "Three veils must be removed from before the Pilgrim's heart ere the Door of Happiness is opened to him. First, that should the dominion of both worlds be offered to him as an eternal gift, he should not rejoice, since whosoever rejoiceth on account of any created thing is still covetous, and the 'covetous man is debarred (from the knowledge of God).' The second veil is this, that should he possess the dominion of both worlds, and should it be taken from him, he should not sorrow for his impoverishment, for this is the sign of wrath, and 'he who is in wrath is tormented.' The third is that he should not be beguiled by any praise or favour, for whosoever is so beguiled is of mean spirit, and such an one is veiled (from the Truth): The Pilgrim must be highminded." Browne, *Literary History of Persia*, Vol. I, p. 425.

does so in his inward and outward aspects, the one and the many. Law is the expression of truth. When we enter into the eternal life of God, we participate in the works of God. While we continue in this unitive state, in God and with God, we also come down to the phenomenal world to fulfil our duties.

The mysticism of Judaism, Christianity and Islam regards the theistic conception of God as determinate and inadequate.

9. RECENT TENDENCIES

There are many leading thinkers born in different religions who are inclined to this great tradition of spiritual religion. F. H. Bradley, in his Introduction to *Appearance and Reality*, says: "Our orthodox theology on the one side and our commonplace materialism on the other side . . . vanish like ghosts before the daylight of free sceptical inquiry." "There is nothing more real than what comes in religion. To compare facts such as these with what is given in outward existence would be to trifle with the subject. The man who demands a reality more solid than that of the religious consciousness seeks, he does not know what," says Bradley.[48] For him reality is experience which is prior to the distinction of self and not-self and prior to any experience which we know as our experience. Bradley is not a solipsist, for the distinction of self and not-self emerges only within the felt unity of experience. Reality is an experience which transcends all relations. Reality satisfies our whole being.[49]

Bergson writes of the soul's immediate union with the

[48] *Appearance and Reality,* p. 449.
[49] Professor C. A. Campbell in his article on "The Metaphysics of Bradley" in the *Church Quarterly Review* (April–June, 1950, p. 41) writes: "Bradley's community of spirit is, I think, with the great mystics of all religions rather than with the orthodox theologians of anyone."

Supreme. The soul "feels an undefinable presence. . . . Then comes a boundless joy, an all-absorbing ecstasy or an all-enthralling rapture. God is there and the soul is in God. Mystery is no more, problems vanish, darkness is dispelled, every thing is flooded in light . . . gone is the distance between the thought and the object of thought, since the problems which measured and indeed constituted the gap, have disappeared. Gone the radical separation between him who loves and him who is beloved. God is there and joy is boundless. . . . The soul becomes in thought and feeling absorbed in God." [50] There is a sudden lifting of the cares of the world, of the burden and anxiety that press on our daily life so steadily that we are unaware of it. We are saved from the dangers of dogmatic belief and dogmatic unbelief. If religion is not to be barren and lifeless, it must get beyond historicity and tradition, and lay stress on the soul "athirst for god." This new temper, this new spirit is on the increase in the living faiths of mankind.

True religion is not what we get from outside, from books and teachers. It is the aspiration of the human soul, that which unfolds within oneself, that which is built by one's life blood. Those who follow this view are the seers. They belong to a single family though they dwell in spaces far apart. They belong to the open, unorganized community, the invisible Church of Spirit, whose membership is scattered over the whole earth. They realise in this world that which is open to man. Their lives are marked by boundless openness, authentic life, fidelity to truth and love for all creation.

[50] *The Two Sources of Morality and Religion*, Eng. translation (1938), pp. 196–7.

L

6

Religious Truth and Symbolism

I. THE METAPHYSICAL DOCTRINE

IN the personal experiences of the seers of the different religions, we discern characteristics which are unaffected by differences of race and geography and which illustrate an astonishing similarity in regard to spiritual life in spite of slight variations. Direct spiritual experience is a psychological state, independent of the metaphysical doctrine which may be derived from the experience. The reality of the experience is not affected by the truth or falsity of the metaphysical doctrine inferred from it. Yet the experience has a cognitive value. It involves a certain metaphysical conception of the nature of the Absolute, the human soul and the world and also a certain way of attaining union with the Absolute or God. There are varieties of expression, variations even among those who profess the same religion. But the similarity is striking whether we take the Hindu seers, the Buddhist teachers, the Greek thinkers like Socrates, Plato, Aristotle and Plotinus, the Christian mystics or the Sufis.

When we reflect on the experience, we leave the sphere of immediacy and begin to discriminate between the experience and what is experienced. We cannot recover the original unity by means of philosophical reflection which interprets the direct experience. The experience cannot be verbalised. Yet as we live in two worlds, the transient and the eternal, we must understand their relationship and express the meaning of the eternal in the terms of the transient.

The interpretation is never adequate to the experience. As all knowledge presupposes the dualism between the subject and the object, we cannot regard man's essential being or the nature of Ultimate Reality as a possible object of cognition. We cannot think of Being as object, for he who thinks and the process of thinking are both immersed in the ocean of Being. To think of Being as object is to do violence to reality and create a fissure between the subject and the object. Being cannot be defined or shown but can only be alluded to, indicated. Yet we think of Being as object, for metaphysics, all these centuries, has been a science of Being. The primordial Being, the primary datum, can be elucidated and not described. To indicate that it is not an object of knowledge, many of the seers refuse to characterise the nature of the Supreme. They declare the Supreme to be a mystery, a hidden secret. The more it is experienced as the inexpressible, the more is it felt to be indubitable. This knowledge does not spring from belief or a process of reasoning. It goes beyond both of them without contradicting them. We can have wordless communion, a transcendental consciousness which exceeds all images and concepts, "a flight of the alone to the Alone."

Many of the seers content themselves with silent adoration and refuse to indulge in words. They describe Him without the sound of words. Bāhva tells his pupil Vāskali that the Self is silence, *śāntoyam ātmā*. St. Augustine says: "God is not even to be called ineffable because to say this is to make an assertion about Him. It is a pure silence, a soundless void." "Wouldst thou be perfect, do not yelp about God," says Eckhart.[1]

There is Absolute Reality, Pure Being with no admixture of matter, with no possibility of change or becoming. He cannot be found in finite things or transitory happenings. He is utterly beyond the here and the now, forever above all that can be seen or imagined, known or named. We can speak of the Absolute only in the negative way. The Absolute Reality with whom the soul seeks to be united is above and beyond all that is finite and concrete. To ascribe any qualities to Him is to limit Him. We can preserve the oneness and wholeness of Infinite Being by eliminating all that is finite. We can only say, not this, not this.

As *Tao Teh Ching* says: "The name that can be named is not the Real Name." Though God comprises Being, he is infinitely beyond it. He is *advaita*, non-dual, beyond every determination or affirmation of any kind. St. Clement says: "God is to be sought in darkness." [2] Again, Pseudo-Dionysius observes: "Unto this Darkness which is beyond light we pray that we

---

[1] Rudolf Otto, *Mysticism, East and West* (1932), p. 7. Cassian describes the ineffability of the experience: "Which transcends all human thoughts and is articulate, I will not say by no sound of the voice, but by no movement of the tongue, or utterance of words; but which the mind, enlightened by the infusion of that heavenly light, describes in no human and confined language, but pours forth richly as from a copious fountain in an accumulation of thoughts, and ineffably utters to God, expressing in the shortest possible space of time such great things that the mind when it returns to its usual conditions cannot easily utter or relate them." *Collation* IX, 25, quoted in Dom Cuthbert Butler, *Benedictine Monachism*, 2nd Ed. (1924), p. 79. In a hymn to Śiva, it is said:
"If even the greatest of the gods, in offering praise,
The hope of comprehending Thee, in full, resign
So may I not be blamed, if, in my humble ways,
I laud Thy name—pardon these stumbling words of mine."
Mahimna Stotra, Eng. translation in *The Light of Truth*, August, 1911, Vol. XII, No. 2.
[2] *Stromata*, I, 2; V, 12.

may come and through loss of sight and knowledge may see and know that which transcends sight and knowledge by the very fact of not seeing and knowing. For this is real sight and knowledge." [3] "The Divine Darkness is the unapproachable light in which God is said to dwell. In this energy one enters who is found worthy to know and to see God by not knowing or seeing him, really being in him who is above sight and knowledge." [4]

According to St. Gregory Palamas, we cannot define God even as Being for he "is beyond every name that can be named and everything that can be thought." For St. Thomas, "the final attainment of man's knowledge of God consists in knowing that we do not know him, insofar as we realise that He transcends everything that we understand concerning Him." [5] "Having arrived at the term of our knowledge we know God as unknown." [6] Eckhart seems to repeat the Upaniṣad phrases: "God is unlike to anything and like to nothing. He is above being. He is the naught." "God is Being itself, without a second, unchangeable, without quality, without form, neither this nor that."

The negative account should not lead us to the suspicion that the Supreme itself is negative. It is the basis of all existent things. So contradictory attributes are given. The Supreme is sometimes viewed as the Super-personal Absolute Godhead or as the Personal God bestowing his love and grace on all the seekers. The metaphysical ideal of the Absolute, transcendent and immanent, gives place in theistic systems to the ideal of God. Prayer takes the place of meditation, and love of knowl-

[3] *Mystical Theology*, II.
[4] *Letters*, V.
[5] *De Potentia*, VII, 5, ad. 14.
[6] *In Boetium de Trinitate*, I, 2, ad. 2.

edge. Liberation becomes life in Heaven. In religious experience we have both knowledge of the Absolute Reality, and personal encounter with God. The two do not exclude each other. Śaṁkara, the famous non-dualist thinker of India, spoke of spiritual union and personal communion. The Old and the New Testaments speak of the religious encounter in personalistic terms. While the personal side is to be met with in Indian religion, there is stress on the highest reality as Absolute Being.

2. THAT ART THOU

The seers of all religions are agreed that there is something in the human soul which is related to the Absolute, which is the Absolute. It is the original ground of the soul, the meeting point of soul and God, the source and basis of all knowledge, all beauty, all goodness, indeed of all ideas of universal significance. The soul can know the Transcendent Reality only because it is one with that Reality, when it descends into its deepest centre. It is there identical with what it knows.

There is a perfect correspondence between the inner nature of man (ātman) and the truth of external reality (Brahman). Man is a microcosm who participates in all strata of the universe, mineral, plant, animal, human and spiritual. All forces are potentially present in him and the universe continues the creative process through him. He has now to shape his world and himself, according to the creative powers he has.

When the Upaniṣads proclaim the great truth "That art thou," [7] when the Buddha teaches that each human individual has in him the power to grow into a Buddha or a Bodhisattva, when the Jews say that the "spirit of man is the candle of the

[7] Compare Madālasā's lullaby to her child: *śuddho'si, buddho'si nirañjano'si.*

Lord," when Jesus tells his hearers that the Kingdom of Heaven is within them and when Muhammad affirms that God is nearer to us than the very artery of our neck, they all mean that the most important thing in life is not to be found in anything external to man but is to be found in the hidden strata of his thought and feeling. We must not look for it, "Lo here or lo there, for behold the Kingdom of God is within you." "Know ye not that ye are the temple of God and that the spirit of God dwelleth in you." [8] In the words of II Peter, we are "partakers of the divine nature." [9] Plotinus tells us that we can know the unknowable, for we ourselves, in our deepest ground, are the unknowable. "This is the soul's true goal, to touch that light and to behold it by means of that light itself, and not by any other light; even as we see not the sun by any light except its own." [10] St. Augustine observes: "Thou art more inward to me than my most inward part." [11] St. Thomas says: "The Holy Ghost inhabits the mind by his substance." [12] Blosius, at the end of the *Book of Spiritual Instruction*, speaks of the hidden essence of the soul.

"It is far more inward and sublime than are the three higher faculties, for it is their origin. It is wholly simple, essential and uniform, and so there is not multiplicity in it, but unity, and in it the three higher faculties are one thing. Here is perfect tranquillity, deepest silence . . . never can any image enter here. By this depth, in which the divine image lies hidden, we are deiform. This same depth is called the heaven of the spirit, for the Kingdom of God is in it. As the Lord said: The Kingdom of

[8] I Corinthians 3:16; see also I Corinthians 6:19; Romans 5:5.
[9] 1:4.
[10] *Enneads*, V. 3. 17.
[11] *Confessions*, III, 11.
[12] *Spiritus sanctus per suam substantiam mentem inhabitat.* C. Gent., IV, 18.

God is within you; and the Kingdom of God is God himself
with all His riches. Therefore this naked and unfigured depth
is above all created things, and is raised above all senses and
faculties; it transcends place and time, abiding by a certain perpetual adhesion in God, its beginning; yet it is essentially within
us, because it is the abyss of the mind and its most inward essence. . . . May God the uncreated Abyss, vouchsafe to call
unto Himself our spirit, the created Abyss, and make it one with
Him, that our spirit plunged in the deep sea of the Godhead
may happily lose itself in the Spirit of God. . . ." [13] St. John
of the Cross says: "Go not to seek Him out of thyself, for that
will be but distraction and weariness, and Thou shalt not find
Him; because there is no fruition of Him more certain, more
ready, more intimate than that which is within." [14] Eckhart
says: "No one can know God who has not first known himself. . . . Since we find God in oneness, that oneness must be
in him who is to find God." Again, "To get at the core of God
at his greatest, one must first get into the core of himself at his
least, for no one can know God who has not first known himself. Go to the depths of the soul . . . to the root, to the
heights; for all that God can do is focussed there." [15] If God
and the human soul were completely different, no amount of
logical reasoning or mediation could lead us to the reality of
God. Goethe said: "If the eye were not sun-like, how could we
ever see light? And if God's own power did not dwell within
us, how could we delight in things divine?" The divine enrap-
tures us because the divine is in us. When the individual self
becomes united with the Self which is the principle of all, there

[13] See Dom Cuthbert Butler, *Western Mysticism* (1922), pp. 305–306.
[14] *The Spiritual Canticle,* Stanza I, 9.
[15] R. Blakney, *Meister Eckhart: A Modern Translation* (1941), Fragment 37; *The Aristocrat,* p. 80, p. 246.

is liberation, the realisation of the self which is calm, serene and undisturbed.

3. RELIGIOUS SYMBOLISM

Hindu thinkers distinguish between *śruti* or the *Veda,* which is independent of any purely human mode of thought and *smṛti* or the tradition, which is based on reasoning and interpretation. The former is the direct expression of the realised truth which proceeds exclusively from the self, which is uncreated and uncreatable. These utterances are supra-individual, universal, divine. They are direct and not discursive. *Anubhava* or direct experience, active participation in the eternal truth, is distinguished from the indirect and passive participation in religious knowledge by belief. In the case of integral insight, the individual does not possess knowledge as an individual but participates in it in his innermost essence, which is not distinct from the divine principle. The metaphysical certitude is absolute because the knower and the known are identical. This is *jñāna,* the most perfect union between God and man.

Its expression does not discuss doubts or answer difficulties. It communicates what is self-evident and certain through symbolical means, which awaken in the reader or hearer the latent knowledge which he bears unconsciously and eternally within him. Intuitive knowledge is symbolical and descriptive. It makes use of rational modes only as symbols to describe or translate absolute knowledge possessing a greater degree of certainty.

When the Vedas, which are the Hindu scriptures, are said to be timeless, the meaning is that the insight into the one Reality is timeless in origin and is unaffected by the human need for diversity of expression. It is this timeless wisdom that the Jews have in view when they say that the Mosaic tradition cannot be annulled. According to Maimonides, the Torah is for all eternity, nothing can be added to it and nothing taken away from it. "For verily I say unto you, till heaven and earth pass, one jot or one tittle shall in no wise pass from the law, till all be fulfilled." [16] "They shall remain there for as long as the heavens and the earth endure, unless thy Lord willeth otherwise." [17] Muhammad was the editor of the Quran. Its substance is uncreated and eternal, subsisting in the essence of the Deity, communicated to the prophet Muhammad by the angel Gabriel. What is timeless is not the literary documents but the wisdom which is available to men of awareness at all times.[18] The inward appropriation of this wisdom may occur in place and time, which may have a great deal to do with the shaping in words of these insights. Human apprehensions of the Eternal enter our ordinary knowledge, assume its forms, become clear to those who have them and are conveyed to others through them. If these apprehensions remained outside the sphere of ordinary knowledge, they would be incapable of communication to others. There is no development in religious truth, though there is a development in the expression of the truth. Excepting a few fundamentalists in each religion, others do not admit the divine authorship of the scriptures and their inerrancy.

The Real has been conceived in many ways through religious

[16] Matthew 5:18.

[17] *Quran* XI, 107.

[18] Dr. Frick of Marburg, in his book *The Gospel, Christianity and Other Faiths* (Eng. translation, 1938) claims absoluteness and finality for the Gospel but not for the historical faiths, including Christianity. "Not only does Christianity share in the inadequacy of other faiths, but it has to face a special condemnation, for through its own fault, it has made unbelievable the preaching of the Gospel." P. 52.

symbolism. We express our felt experience in propositions that are symbolical and descriptive. We communicate the experience to those who have not had it through what is already known to them. A true symbol is not a dream or a shadow. It is the living revelation of the Unfathomable. The Vedic Aryans and the followers of Zarathustra look upon fire (agni) as the symbol of the Supreme. The brightness of the Unmitigated Reality suggests to us the image of the burning fire. The Upaniṣad calls it the light of lights, *jyotiṣām jyotiḥ*. Boehme and William Law speak of it as the Divine Light.[19]

A familiar human relationship is used for defining the relation of man to God. God is father. The Vedas and the Upaniṣads use it. It comes out prominently in Jesus' teaching. In agony at Gethsemane he cried: "Abba, Father." [20] A saying is attributed to him: "Father, forgive them. . . . Father, into thy hands, I commit my spirit." [21] To his disciples he says: "When ye pray, say our Father." [22]

The different symbolical representations bring out varied aspects of the immensity of the Supreme. Thomas Aquinas adopted from Aristotle the principle of "analogy" or a measure of likeness between man and God, between human reason and Divine Truth. So he argues that in Natural Religion, or what man can acquire for himself by means of his own reason, there are certain elements of truth, which are partial and so

[19] Goethe's letter to Jacobi, January 6, 1813: "With all the manifold facets of my being, one way of thinking is not sufficient for me; as a poet and artist I am a polytheist, but a pantheist as a student of nature, and either belief I hold with equal determination. And if I need a divinity for my personal being, my moral existence—well, this need, too, is promptly catered for." Erich Heller, *The Disinherited Mind* (1952), p. 40.

[20] Mark 14:36.

[21] Luke 23:34, 46.

[22] Matthew 6:9.

need completion by truths of revelation. Our concepts present the truth to our minds in a mode that falls infinitely short of the reality of God. We accept the dogma or the symbol through faith, which is for most people the only possible mode of participation in the divine truth. The forms and symbols are ways to help us to an inward realisation. All the time, the seers are aware that human language breaks down when it attempts to expound the nature of Ultimate Reality. Knowledge does not pretend to leave nothing unexplained. Its limitations are so obvious that a complete and final explanation of the nature of reality condemns itself by its very claim to completeness and finality. However perfect and final the revelation may be, when once it enters the realm of human apprehension, it is subject to all the imperfections of the human mind. To claim finality or infallibility for human pictures of reality is to claim for man what belongs to God. If anyone tells us that his view of the Supreme is final, it is a human judgment which need not be taken as infallible.

The variety of symbolism is due, not to the nature of the experience as such, but to the prevailing theological or metaphysical conceptions of time and place. These colour the expectation of the seer and form the background through which he interprets his illumination.

> Life, like a dome of many-colored glass,
> Stains the white radiance of eternity.
>
> Shelley.

Again, as another poet says:

> For every fiery prophet in Old times
> And all the sacred madness of the bard,
> When God made music through him,

Could but make his music by the framework
   and the chord.

"The framework and the chord" give shape and form to the experience, especially when it is reported and interpreted.

It is wrong to exaggerate the doctrinal differences, overlooking the common basis, the universal fact underlying the historical formulations. The diversity of dogmatic interpretations tends to diminish as we climb up the ladder of spiritual perfection. If we leave aside the secondary interpretations, we find that the seers make practically the same report about the nature of Absolute Reality.[23]

The symbols and dogmas are not definitive. Eastern forms of religion hold that differences of interpretation do not affect the one universal truth any more than the differences of colours affect the uncoloured light which is transmitted. Western forms of religion are inclined to hold that one definition is final and absolute and others are false. In India, each definition represents a *darśana* or a viewpoint. There are many ways of viewing one experience. The different *darśanas* are different viewpoints which are not necessarily incompatible. They are pointers on the way to spiritual realisation. If religious truth is seen by different groups in different ways, it is not to deny that truth is ultimately one. If there are resemblances in higher

[23] Ruysbroeck says: "[In the reality experienced by the mystic] we can speak no more of Father, Son and Holy Spirit, nor of any creature, but only of one Being, which is the very substance of the Divine Person. There were we all one before our creation, for this is our super-essence. There the Godhead is in simple essence without activity." A devout Catholic of the Counter Reformation period, I. I. Olier observes: "The holy light of faith is so pure, that compared with it, particular lights are but impurities; and even ideas of the saints, of the Blessed Virgin, and the sight of Jesus Christ in his humanity are impediments in the way of the sight of God in His purity."

religions, they are to be welcomed as the expressions of the working of the mysterious spirit of God at sundry times and in diverse manners, binding them all together in a single whole. For the judgments of the well-instructed and virtuous men are to be trusted in matters of religion. The Hindu doctrines of *adhikāra,* spiritual competence, and *iṣta-devatā,*[24] chosen deity, proceed on the assumption that the discipline prescribed for any individual should have relevance to his spiritual growth.

In the *Ṛg. Veda,* in the *Upaniṣads,* in the *Bhagavadgītā,* the freedom to worship God in the form that must appeal to us is permitted. For they see the transcendent spiritual aim of all historical religions. They hold that all paths lead to the summit. "As men approach me so do I accept them. Men on all sides follow my path." [25] God is leading all the people of

---

[24] *Mahābhārata* shows "that people of low caste, enemies and foreigners were received into the Hindu fold. . . . A passage of Patañjali attests that the Śakas and the Yāvanas could perform sacrifices and accept food from an Ārya without contaminating it. The fact is that Hinduism is a way of life, a mode of thought, that becomes second nature. It is not so much its practices that are important, for they can be dispensed with; nor is it the Church, since it has no priesthood, or at least no sacerdotal hierarchy. The important thing is to accept certain fundamental conceptions, to acknowledge a certain "spirituality," a term much abused in current parlance. For many Hindus it would be quite legitimate to take Jesus as *iṣta-devatā* without even regarding Him as an *avatāra,* so long as Indian tradition were acknowledged." Louis Renou, *Religions of Ancient India* (1953), pp. 55–56.

[25] *Bhagavadgītā* (IV. 11.).

    yenākāreṇa ye martyāḥ mām evaikam upāsate
    tenākāreṇa tebhyoham prapanno vāñchitam dade.
     vidhinā avidhinā vāpi bhaktyā ye (martyāḥ) mām upāsate
    tebhyaḥ phalam prayacchāmi, prapanno'ham na saṁśayaḥ.

Śiva Gītā, XII, 5–6. "There exist," says Origen, "diverse forms of the Word under which It reveals itself to Its disciples, conforming Itself to the degree of light of each one, according to the degree of their progress in saintliness." *Contra Celsum,* IV, 16.

Meister Eckhart says: "God never tied man's salvation to any pattern. Whatever possibilities inhere in any pattern of life inhere in all, because

the world on to the fulness of life by diverse paths. The resources of release are available to all, though all may not appropriate them equally. God has no special favourites. "I am
alike to all beings." "None is hateful or dear to me. But those
who worship me with devotion are in me and I in them."
There is a wider divine fellowship which includes the different
religious groups. The Hindu attitude on this matter is not the
result of lazy indifference to truth but the outcome of sincere
love of truth.

When the symbol loses its character and becomes a dogma,
it engenders unbelief. Jesus said: "Woe unto you, lawyers! for
ye have taken away the key of knowledge; ye enter not in
yourselves and them that were entering in, ye hindered." [26]
When the Buddha repudiated the Veda, it was the sterile ceremonialism to which the great truths were reduced that he
criticized. When St. Paul rejected the Jewish Law, it was the
pharisaical formalism lacking spiritual life that he rejected.
Absolute truth is beyond all its possible expressions. The expressions are limited as their differentiation and multiplicity
illustrate. Every expression of the truth is relative. It cannot
possess a unique value to the exclusion of others. It cannot be
the only possible expression of what it expresses. Any specific
form is by hypothesis limited and so leaves something outside
itself.

Those who adopt a particular form and have not reached
the formless truth are inclined to regard their relative truth as
absolute and confuse eternal truths with historic facts. The
different religions are like various languages in which God has
spoken to man.

God has given it so and denied it to none. One good way does not conflict with another . . . for not all people may travel the same road."
[26] Luke 11:52.

7

God-Realisation and the Way to It

1. SPIRITUAL REBIRTH

EASTERN religions are distinguished by the emphasis they lay on experience rather than on authority. They have their rituals and mythologies but the basic conception that dominates their whole history is the renewal of consciousness. The aim of religion is not intellectual conformity to inherited doctrine or mild ritualistic piety. The purpose of religion is spiritual, and not merely metaphysical conversion. It is the displacement of ignorance, *avidyā*, unawareness, by knowledge, *vidyā* or awareness. This attainment of *vidyā, bodhi,* wisdom or enlightenment makes for power, conviction. It results in a complete renewing of one's nature, which is assimilated to the new inward dimension. We feel at home in the world. There is no feeling of estrangement but one of restored harmony. All things are of one piece, Mokṣa, Nirvána, the Kingdom of God are inward states of mind. He who has succeeded in attaining the aim of religion has an illumined mind, a changed heart and a transformed will. A new way of life vitalises and transforms one's whole being. This is *dvitīyam janma,* the second birth. "There is a new creation; behold all things are become new." The lotus which is generally used in Hindu and Buddhist thought as an offering to the divine is symbolic of the effort we have to make to wrest the utmost of glorifying beauty from our chaotic passions.

This world has its root above and branches below, says the *Bhagavadgītā*.[1] "I am from above; ye are of this world." These passages suggest that the perception of the truth is derived from the nature in us which is above the earthly. Spiritual power from beyond the dimensions of space-time breaks in. Man is the point of interaction between time and eternity. The *Bhagavadgītā* makes out that the religious man is awake while the rest of the world is asleep.[2] We are said to be asleep so long as the spell of the material world lasts. We continue to live our life in a routine way. We are born, earn a living, raise a family, take part in politics or business, age and die. There is nothing wrong in doing these things; only the awakened soul does these things with the perspective of the eternal.

This, to my mind, is the teaching of Christianity. The saving knowledge of God is not knowledge of and faith in Jesus as a historic person portrayed in the Gospels. Christ is not to be equated with the historic Jesus.[3] Christ is the spirit of the Supreme, the Eternal Word. The manifestation of this Word in history is not limited to Jesus. Salvation is mediated through the Eternal Christ, the Word of God which is not to be confused with the historic Jesus. It is open to those who have not heard of him and are yet loyal to the spirit of truth. The Fourth Gospel tells us that the Word of God that tabernacled among us in Jesus had also been operative in all creation from

[1] XV, 1.
[2] II, 69.
[3] Cf. Kierkegaard: "History has nothing whatever to do with Christ." T. H. Croxall, *Kierkegaard Studies* (1948).
Emil Brunner remarks: "Christian faith is not interested in the Founder of Christianity." *The Mediator*, Eng. translation (1934), p. 81.

M

the very beginning [4] and is the "light that enlighteneth every man." [5] St. Paul affirms that centuries before the birth of Jesus, Christ was with the Israelites during their wanderings in Sinai. "They drank of a spiritual Rock that followed them; and that Rock was Christ." [6] Justin Martyr claims that philosophers like Socrates and Heraclitus were essentially Christians since they lived for the truth and Christ is truth. All who strive wholeheartedly for truth were welcomed by him as fellow Christians. Augustine says: "That which today is called Christian religion existed among the Ancients and has never ceased to exist from the origin of the human race until the time when Christ himself came and men began to call Christian the true religion which already existed beforehand." [7] Christian religion is the continuation and restoration of the ancient religions, of something eternal, the Law which Christ came to fulfil but not to destroy. The means of salvation is essentially always the same, though its modes may vary in accordance with the different ethnical and cultural environments to which it reveals itself. To be a Christian is not the profession of an outward creed but the living of an inward life.

When, according to the Fourth Gospel, Jesus says, "I am come that they might have life and have it more abundantly," he means that he opens the eyes of men, quickens their sensitiveness, arouses them from their sleep, discloses to them the reality of the Eternal dwelling in them. This is to be born again. The idea of rebirth into the world of spirit is mentioned in St. Paul's letter to the Ephesians. [8] "Put off your old nature which belongs to your former manner of life and is corrupt

[4] John 1: 1–3.
[5] John 1:9.
[6] I Corinthians 10:4.
[7] *Retract*, I, XIII, 3.
[8] 4:22–24. George Fox, the founder of the Society of Friends, once

through deceitful lusts and be renewed in the spirit of your minds, and put on the new nature, created after the likeness of God in true righteousness and holiness." The rebornness or putting on the new nature involves struggle. The Buddha had to overcome Māra, Zoroaster Ahriman and Jesus Satan.

How are we to attain the rebornness, the total unselfness? How are we to overcome our corrupt nature, our selfish ambitions? He who suffers from egoism boasts, "These sons belong to me, and this wealth belongs to me. With such thoughts a fool is tormented. He himself does not belong to himself; how much less sons and wealth?" [9] Jesus says: "Whoso loveth his life loseth it, whoso hateth his life in this world keeps it into life eternal." There is an anonymous Christian saying: "Nothing burns in hell save self-will." We must die in order to live. The change involves a break with the past. To shake off the prides and jealousies, the intellectual conceits is painful. The way to perfection is described as steep and hard, lonely and arduous, as sharp as the edge of a razor. The way is described as consisting of steps or ascents which are variously described as the purgative, the illuminative and the unitive stages. The emphasis may be on the emotional or the volitional or the cognitive aspects. We may reach the end through devotion, meritorious action and intellectual contemplation. These are not exclusive; they interpenetrate.

2. THE WAY OF DEVOTION: BHAKTI MĀRGA

Of the different ways by which we can centre our lives in the Supreme, the way of devotion, the *bhakti mārga* is accessible to the poor and the illiterate, to the high and the low. It

said: "You say that Christ said this and the Apostles said that but what do you say?" When Jesus says: "I say unto you," he is speaking from his inward experience.

[9] *Dhammapada*, V, 62.

is the path of devotion to God and submission to his will. The
principal centre of spiritual life is the heart. By inward prayer,
we enable the heart to participate in the union with God. To
be a Muslim is to submit to the will of God, to be guided by
universal purpose, not selfish interest. By devotion and prayer
we attain a state of mind in which we become detached from
everything pertaining to the world and are directly united with
God. Bhakti includes faith and love.

The invocation of the Divine Name is a part of the spiritual
movement of bhakti. The Hindu *Japa,* the Buddhist *bud-
dhānusmṛti* and the Muslim *dhikr* refer to the invocation of
the Divine Name. For the Jews, "The name of the Lord is a
strong tower; the righteous runneth into it and is safe." The
prophet Joel says: "Whosoever shall call on the name of the
Lord shall be delivered." "The Name of Jesus," says St. Bernard, "is not only light; it is also nourishment. All food is too
dry to be assimilated by the soul if it is not first flavoured by
this condiment; it is too insipid unless this salt relieves its taste-
lessness. I have no taste for thy writings, if I cannot read this
Name there; no taste for thy discourse, if I do not hear it re-
sounding therein. It is honey for my mouth, melody for my
ears, joy for my heart, but it is also medicine. Does any one
among you feel overcome with sadness? Let him then taste
Jesus in his mouth and heart, and behold how, before the light
of His Name, all clouds vanish and the sky again becomes
serene. Has one among you allowed himself to be led into a
fault, and is he experiencing the temptation of despair? Let
him invoke the Name of the Life and the Life will restore
him." [10] Gandhi's Rāmdhūn assumes that God bestows his

[10] Sermon 15 on the Song of Songs.

grace on those who invoke his name with utter faith and sincerity.[11]

As a result of devotion to God, one attains the state of bliss.[12]

The Christian way is pre-eminently the way of devotion. It is analogous to the Mahāyāna Buddhist and the Hindu bhakti movements.

Muhammad prescribes prayer, fasting, almsgiving, pilgrimages and ablutions. Prayer will carry the seeker halfway to God, fasting will bring him to the door of his palace and almsgiving will gain him admittance. Every Muslim is a priest and there is no need for a mediator. In prayer, the Muslim is enjoined to direct his eyes and thoughts towards a visible point of the horizon, to the holy temple of Mecca, though every spot is equally pure. Though all days are equally good, Friday is set apart for public worship. We have seen Muslims prostrate themselves unself-consciously on the remote hills or in the market place.

In theistic religions, we look upon the Supreme as our Father and Creator and pray for his grace. If the Supreme is viewed as the Absolute Reality, sin is not disobedience but alienation from one's true being and we regain peace by meditation. By prayer to God we seek his grace. In *The Spirit of Prayer*, William Law observes: "The sun meets not the springing bud that stretches towards it with half that certainty as God, the source of all good, communicates himself to the soul that longs to partake of Him."

[11] D. T. Suzuki in his *Essays in Zen Buddhism* (Vol. III) says: "The original vow of Amida is 'to receive in his land of Felicity whoever shall pronounce His Name with absolute confidence: happy then are those who pronounce His Name. A man may possess faith, but if he does not pronounce the Name, his faith will be of no use to him."

[12] *Yoga Sūtra*, II, 45.

3. THE WAY OF ACTION: KARMA MĀRGA

Man, as he is, is a composite of different elements which call for reconciliation. He is capable of sublime goodness and intense evil, of charity and of hatred, of reverence for suffering and of ruthlessness which inflicts pain. As he is, he is a pathological creature. Evil is due to the hardness of the human heart, and wilful disobedience. The *Mahābhārata* says: "I know the right but I do not wish to engage in it; I know the wrong, but I do not wish to refrain from it." [13] The same human experience is expressed by St. Paul: "For the good which I would I do not; but the evil which I would not, that I practise." That man's nature is divided is a manifest fact of experience. His nature is not wholly corrupt. Were it so, there would be no hope or possibility of any improvement. The *Bhagavadgītā* opens with a conflict where Arjuna appeals to the voice of the Divine in him, the God in the chariot, the same voice which was heard in the story of the Garden of Eden. When temptation issued in sin and sin in shame, Adam heard the voice, "What is this that thou hast done?"

All life is a continuous struggle with temptation and evil. The more we overcome the temptation the greater is the happiness of achievement. We can overcome temptation only by disciplined effort. Tension between flesh and spirit is a prominent feature of the New Testament. St. Paul writes: "Walk in the Spirit and ye shall not fulfil the lusts of the flesh. The flesh lusteth against the Spirit and the Spirit against the flesh." The flesh does not mean the physical body, which is an inescapable condition of man's life on earth. The body is to serve a positive purpose. When the Christian doctrine affirms that "the Word became flesh," it is evident that "flesh" is not in-

[13] jānāmi dharmaṁ na ca me pravṛttiḥ
jānāmi adharmaṁ na ca me nivṛttiḥ.

trinsically evil. Flesh and spirit do not stand for the physical
and the non-physical aspects of human nature. The body is
neutral ground. By walking in the spirit we overcome the
limitations of the body. The body is the raw material which a
spirit-filled life uses for spiritual development. A carna -minded
person may abuse his body. Man is a duality. The more he
overcomes the temptations of the flesh the nearer he comes to
his goal.

Brahmacarya or abstinence from physical pleasures is insisted on. The breaking down of strong habitual barriers requires effort; vigilance is also needed as these habits tend to
re-form quickly.

"A man's life consisteth not in the abundance of the things
which he possesseth." The more we depend on the mechanical
devices whose smooth functioning enables us to live a life of
comfort at the material level, the more estranged do we become from an awareness of inner reality. We are called upon
to cultivate a spirit of detachment. By the spirit of renunciation we can purify ourselves. "Neither by work, nor through
progeny, nor through wealth but by renunciation alone is life
eternal reached." [14] According to the *Kūṭadanta Sutta,* the
Buddha says: "Greater than the sacrifice of animals is the
sacrifice of the self. He who offers to the gods his sinful desires
will see the uselessness of slaughtering animals at the altar.
Blood has no cleansing power, but the rooting out of lust will
make the heart pure. Better than worshipping gods is obedience to the laws of righteousness." St. Paul in Romans says:
"For if you live according to the flesh you will die, but if by
the Spirit you put to death the deeds of the body, you will

[14] na karmaṇā na prajayā dhanena tyāgenaike amṛtatvam ānaśuḥ.
Mahānārāyaṇa Upaniṣad, VIII, 14.

live." [15] We become "heirs of God and fellow heirs with Christ, provided we suffer with him in order that we may also be glorified with him." [16] So the Apostle adds: "I appeal to you, therefore, brethren, by the mercies of God, to present your bodies as a living sacrifice, holy and acceptable to God, which is your spiritual worship." [17]

To have greater opportunities of self-control, men sometimes retire from the world. From very early times we have had monastic orders in Hinduism and Buddhism. The monastic orders of Christianity derive from the desert fathers, the Apostles and Jesus. A monastic order, the Cistercian order, so called from the original abbey of Citeaux, founded in Burgundy in 1098, established monasteries in solitary places. Their inmates led simple and laborious lives. The most illustrious figure of the order was the founder of Clairvaux, St. Bernard. Monastic life is, in the Rule of St. Benedict, the "commencement of religious life" while for "him who hastens his steps towards the perfection of monastic life, there are the teachings of the Holy Fathers, the carrying out of which leads man to the supreme end of religion." Monastic life itself is not the summit of spiritual perfection. Muhammad prescribes a fast of thirty days which is meant to subdue the body and purify the soul.

A life of contemplation does not aim at complete separation from the world. It uses material things as means to spiritual ends. It does not deny rights to the body but strives to use the body to shape the soul. This is possible only if the soul cleanses itself from external stains and strips off its own lower nature. [18]

[15] 8:13.
[16] 8:17.
[17] 12:1, 3.
[18] "Chisel away from the soul what is superfluous, straighten that which

Each individual is infinitely precious in God's eyes, whatever be his rank or position in society. By contemplation we develop a deep sense of piety towards life. We can improve the social order only when we wholeheartedly strive for justice and equality for all and accept individual responsibility for achieving this end. Listen to the prophet repeating the words of God. "And I shall make justice the rule and righteousness the standard." [19] This is the other part of his message: "Cease to do evil, learn to do good. Practice justice. Hold in check the oppressor. Secure the right of the fatherless. Plead the cause of the widow." [20]

The Buddha asks us to cultivate love for all beings. He says: "Our mind shall not waver, no vile speech will we utter; we will abide, tender and compassionate, loving in heart, void of secret malice; and we will be ever suffusing such a one with the rays of our loving thought, and from him forthgoing, we will be ever suffusing the whole world with thought of love far-reaching, grown great and beyond measures, void of ill-will and bitterness." [21] "As a mother at the risk of her life protects her own child, her only child, so also let every one cultivate good will towards all beings." [22] Of the many Buddhas, Amitābha (Amida in Japan) is one of the most popular. He was once a monk who, ages ago, took forty-six vows out of love for his fellow beings. He resolved to devote all his wisdom and merit to the saving of others. Amitābha is the perfect embodi-

---

is crooked, purify and enlighten that which is dark, and do not cease working at thy statue until virtue shines before thine eyes with its divine splendour, and thou seest temperance seated in thy bosom in its holy purity." Plotinus, *Enneads*, I, 6, 9.

[19] Isaiah 28:17.
[20] Isaiah 1:17.
[21] *Majjhina Nikāya.*
[22] *Metta Sutta.*

ment of wisdom and mercy. Whoever meditates on him with devotion is assured of entry into Paradise through receiving a portion of the saviour's tremendous treasury of merit. The doctrine of *parivarta* or turning over of merit to the advantage of others points to the interdependence of all life.

Jesus says: "Ye have heard that it hath been said, Thou shalt love thy neighbour, and hate thine enemy. But I say unto you, Love your enemies." [23] "If a man say, I love God, and hateth his brother, he is a liar; for he that loveth not his brothers whom he hath seen, how can he love God whom he hath not seen? And this commandment have we from him, that he who loveth God love his brother also." [24]

The City of God has for its counterpart the City of Men and the latter can only be a universal human society founded on a belief in the same fundamental vision of the common good and indeed upon a certain communion in things of the spirit.

4. THE WAY OF KNOWLEDGE: JÑĀNA MĀRGA

By speculative knowledge we get to the gates of reality but we cannot enter Truth by means of thought alone. It can be reached only through the perfection of the whole human nature. If we are to transcend the limitations of human nature, we must practise the virtues of body, mind and spirit. To look upon the body as the source and principle of evil is an error akin to manichaeism. Man is not a spiritual being temporarily confined within the prison of the body, a stranger in an alien world. He is a part of nature, that dynamic order which embraces all existence from inorganic matter to spiritual beings.

[23] Matthew 5:43.
[24] I John 4:20–21.

Spirit is the aim of nature, the principle of human responsibility. Even as the soul is the form of the body, the City of God,
brahma-loka is the form, the goal of this universe. The obstacle
to the perfecting of man is not the body but the spirit inciting
to evil. The body is the house of God, *devālaya,* a "tabernacle
of the Holy Spirit."

The control of passions does not mean their annihilation but
their transmutation into spiritual energy. The body can here
and now participate in the life of the spirit. A sanctified body
can express the Divine.

The divine seed is in us. It has to be allowed to grow up.
We have intimations of a larger awareness than we have yet
realised. "And the light shineth in darkness and the darkness comprehendeth it not." The shell must be broken, if
the living kernel is to be reached. If we are to reach the light,
we must put out the darkness. We must descend to the quiet
mysterious depths and penetrate through quietude, not the
illusory quietude of idleness and the void of thought but the
infinite quietude in which all the energies are at play. Contemplation is not emptiness of mind or the absence of all
thought. We hold the mind away from the undertakings and
fictions of the world, let it sink deep into abstraction and lead
it to reach and enjoy a tranquillising spirit of freedom from
the pressure of life and work. This state of poise can be reached
only by vigorous effort.

Yoga aims at the reintegration of the self. It is a kind of in-
gathering, recollecting, a concentrated relating of self to self
when we realise the powers of the self. The term yoga suggests
techniques and disciplines which are to be found in different
degrees in all religions. Yoga is *citta-vṛtti-nirodha* or the stilling of all mental activities. This stilling of the activities leads

us to the mind itself, which is the source and condition of all activity, in its original state. There is a mind in man immeasurably superior to the ordinary mind.[25] With the upper surface of the mind we articulate thoughts; deep down is the region where we meditate. We imagine that inspiration comes from above the soul; it comes from within the soul, from above conceptual reason. To get into the depths we must practise silent meditation. In that process we are alone but not lonely. In that solitude we perceive the power which gives confidence in spite of the presence of the negativities of existence.[26] It is difficult to continue the practice of meditation for long. St. Gregory the Great refers to the passage in the Apocalypse: "There was silence in heaven about half an hour" and comments: "For heaven is the soul of the righteous. When therefore the quiet of contemplation takes place in the mind, there is silence in heaven. . . . But because this quiet of the mind cannot be perfect in this life, it is not said that there was silence in heaven a whole hour, but about half an hour; because as soon as the mind begins to raise itself, and to be

[25] Plato writes in the *Phaedo* (79): "The soul, when using the body as an instrument of perception, that is to say, when using the sense of sight or hearing or some other sense, is dragged by the body into the region of the changeable and wanders and is confused. But when returning to herself she reflects, then she passes into the other world, the region of purity and eternity and immortality and unchangeableness which are her kindred, and with them she ever lives when she is by herself and is not let or hindered; then she ceases from her erring ways, and being in communion with the unchanging, is unchanging. And this state of the soul is called wisdom."

[26] St. Gregory says: "Inward knowledge is not cognisable unless there is a cessation from outward embarrassments, and our mind is never caught up to the force of inward contemplation, unless it be first carefully lulled to rest from all agitation of earthly desires." (*Morals in Job*, V, 55.) Again: "The voice of God is heard when, with minds at ease, we rest from the bustle of this world, and the divine precepts are pondered by us in the deep silence of the mind." (*Ibid.*, XXIII, 27.)

inundated with the light of interior quiet, the turmoil of thoughts soon comes back, and it is thrown into disorder from itself, and being disordered it is blinded." [27]

The *Yoga Sūtra* helps us to develop a single-minded concentration on the Supreme. It asks us to be still, to cease from struggle, to wait and let the light within shine forth. It assumes that the soul is the vehicle of the Spirit even as the body is the vehicle of the soul.

Concentration may be attained by fixing the mind on the Inner Light, which is beyond sorrow, or on the heart of an illumined soul that is free from passion or on any divine form or symbol that appeals to one as good. [28] Concentration is not a swoon or a trance. It is an act of close attention. Plotinus asks us to take the inward way, lay aside all that is other than God and in the solitude of the self "behold that solitary dwelling existence, the Apart, the Unmingled, the Pure, that upon which all things depend, for which all look and live and act and know, the source of life and of Intellection and of Being." [29]

We take up a familiar passage or mantra and, meditating on it, the soul waits in silence and makes itself into a shrine where God dwells. God makes himself felt as the sure foundation of all life and in all his frailty man surrenders himself to him. When we are face to face with God in all his holiness, we are lost in adoration of him as we know that he is above all praise.

Contemplation is our freedom in the very awareness of universal bondage. It is the witness to the self which is above the stream of necessities. Liberty is found in the self, however

[27] Dom Cuthbert Butler, *Western Mysticism* (1922), p. 94–5.
[28] *Yoga Sūtra*, I, 36–39.
[29] *Enneads*, I, 6, 7.

painful the outward conditions may be. In the state of samādhi or transcendental consciousness we encounter the Unconditioned Being with our total being. If we commit ourselves to the pursuit of supreme truth with joyous abandon, unexpected insights, new experiences of spiritual power and freedom arise, which will bring light and inspiration to every sphere of our activity. Arguments give us assurance but experience produces certainty. When, as the result of the Yoga discipline, body, mind, feelings and intuitions are reconciled, when the individual secures wholeness and balance, he becomes a channel through which the Universal in us expresses itself unobstructedly.

Thanks to the work of the Society of Friends in the West, silent worship has entered into the practice of the Western churches. There is a room set apart for meditation in the United Nations building in New York City though I am not sure that it is made use of very much. Pascal's saying that the whole of man's misery comes from his inability to stay quietly in a room by himself is well known. All religions ask us to listen in silent contemplation to the voice of the Divine.

To a generation like the present which is battered by so many anxieties and distracted by so many noises, the cultivation of silence will be a great corrective. It will show up the complacency and hypocrisy of an attitude of mind which comprises a tenacious property sense, moral lawlessness, greed of pleasure and erotic despair.

5. TRUTH AND LOVE

Being and becoming are not separated from each other. A life in spirit expresses itself in love for then we will know one another and love one another in that which is Eternal. We interpret and express the truth we have attained in what we are, think and do in the present world. Though the earthbound life is not all and in it nothing abides, we can enjoy and extend relationships over which death has no power.[30] The light within is universal. Every man has it. The image of God may be defiled or weakened but it cannot be totally obliterated for it belongs to the very constitution of man. There is hope for the worst sinner, the darkest criminal. There is no such thing as hell. We cannot believe that God has rejected hosts of men and women to eternal death. The light within summons all to peace, serenity and joy.

The notion of the elect people of God is repudiated by this view. All those who consciously obey the light are saved. Those who do not are the world yet to be saved; they are not lost. When we see the Universal Spirit of Truth in each individual, we will love the meanest of creation as oneself. This is the golden rule taught by all religions.

The Hindu epic, *Mahābhārata* says: "In joy and sorrow, in pleasure and pain, one should act towards others as one would have them act toward oneself." [31] The trees bear fruits, the rivers carry waters, the cows give milk, and good men live for the good of others.[32]

Confucius, when asked, "Is there a maxim which one may observe as a rule of conduct for life?" replied: Is not this to be found in the word, *shu,* i.e., to act to others as one would act toward oneself, or as this is translated by his disciple Tseng Tze, "to love others with the heart with which one loves oneself."

[30] Cf. "Let your light so shine before men that they may see your good works." Matthew 5:16.

[31] XII, 113, 9.

[32] paropakārāya phalanti vṛkṣāḥ, paropakārāya vahanti nadyāḥ paropakārāya duhanti gāvāḥ paropakārāya satāṁ hi jīvanam.

"Love thy neighbour as thyself," found in the nineteenth chapter of the Book of Leviticus is said to be the one commandment which transcends all the 613 commandments of the Bible. The prophet Hosea spoke of love, mercy and forgiveness. He forgave his erring wife: because he loved her and therefore assumed that God would forgive humanity because he loves it. The Mosaic law proclaims that there shall be one law for the stranger and for the home born, for "Remember ye were strangers in the land of Egypt." In the Old Testament we read "Have we not one Father? Has not one God created us all?" According to Hillel, "what is hateful to you do not do to your fellow-creature." [33]

Ahiṁsā or non-violence or, positively put, love for all creation is the central feature of the Jaina faith. The Buddha, after attaining enlightenment, spent the rest of his life teaching friends the way to realise the blissful experience of Nirvána. Mātṛceta describes Buddha in these words: "Towards an enemy intent on ill, you are a friend intent on good; even in a constant faultseeker you are bent on searching for virtues." [34] Śāntideva describes the Bodhisattva ideal in beautiful words:

In reward for all this righteousness that I have won by my works, I would fain become a soother of all the sorrows of all creatures.

May I be a balm to the sick, their healer and servitor, until sickness come never again.

May I quench with rains of food and drink the anguish of hunger and thirst. May I be, in the famine at the ages' end, their drink and meat.

[33] *Sab.* 31a.
[34] ahitāvahite śatrau tvam hitāvahitaḥ suhṛt
doṣānveṣaṇanitye'pi guṇānveṣaṇatatparaḥ.

May I become an unfailing store for the poor, and serve them with manifold things for their need.

My own being and my pleasures, all my righteousness in the past, present or future I surrender indefinitely, that all creatures may win to their end.

The Stillness lies in surrender of all things, and my spirit is fain for the Stillness. If I must surrender all, it is best to give it for fellow-creatures.

I yield myself to all living things to deal with me as they list; they may smite or revile me for ever, bestrew me with dust, play with my body, laugh and wanton; I have given them my body, why shall I care?

May all who slander me, or do me hurt, or jeer at me, gain a share in the Enlightenment.

I would be a protector of the unprotected, a guide to wayfarers, a ship, a dyke, and a bridge for them who seek the further Shore; a lamp for them who need a lamp, a bed for them who need a bed, a slave for all beings who need a slave.[35]

In the Gospel of Matthew it is said: "Whatever you wish that men would do to you, do so to them." It is not enough to "love them which love you"; it is more important to "love your enemies . . . do good to them that hate you and pray for them which despitefully use you and persecute you."[36]

Sādi writes: "Behold the generosity and grace of the Lord; the slave has sinned, yet he bears the shame."[37]

Farid, if a man beat thee,

[35] *The Path of Light,* Eng. translation by L. D. Barnett (1947), pp. 44–5, 48–9.
[36] Matthew 5:44.
[37] *Kullīyāt. Gulistān.*

N

Beat him not in return, but kiss his feet.
Farid, if thou long for the Lord of all,
Become as grass for men to tread on.
Farid, when one man breaketh thee,
And another trampleth on thee,
Then shalt thou enter the court of the Lord.[38]

6. SANCTITY AND LIFE IN THE WORLD

Sanctity is the evidence of authentic religious spirit. It is found in every age and in every religion. The holy men are indifferent to considerations of worldly prestige that normally weigh with ordinary people. They belong to a different kind of world. In spite of their diversity of temperament and calling, a Francis of Assisi, a Rāmakrsna, a Gandhi have striking family resemblance. They are characterised by a profound insight into human nature, penetration of shams, and consuming love of God and man.

The saint is not liberated from action on this earth. He does not leave behind the concrete world of finite values and meanings. His self is not lost by participation in the life of the Divine. Only he becomes not merely a part of the world but the ground of the whole. As he has a body, he is not entirely freed from the distinction of good and evil. The Supreme acts through the power of the individual selves; it does not swallow them up. Morality for the redeemed is, in its own order, a reflection of spirituality. The saint is ever ready to bring a cup of water to his sick brethren. Every occasion of the world is a means for transfiguring insight and active charity, when we feel ourselves to be one with the universe, when in the words of Traherne, "the sea flows in our veins . . . and the stars

[38] *Granth Sahib,* quoted by C. F. Andrews in *The Student Movement,* Oct., 1909.

are our jewels." When all things are perceived as holy, there is no room for covetousness or self-assertion, or the pursuit of power or dreary pleasures.

When one gives up all things in spirit, all things belong to one in a new dimension. One does not disown the things of the world but possesses them with an inner detachment and so a fresh delight. The reborn souls living in peace and complete self-possession share with the Divine the task of reclaiming and redeeming the world. They take up the burden of the world even as "the bees make honey or the spiders secrete filaments." They do not love their family, creed, community or nation. They love their kind. Their lives are the outward and visible signs of something in them which passes present understanding, which is not temporal but eternal. The work for the world's welfare is imposed on them. The bodhisattva of the Mahāyāna philosophy, though he is not under the constraint of the law of karma, lives in the world working for the redemption of suffering creatures, for all creation is bound together. "Necessity is laid upon me," says St. Paul. Luther asserts: "Here I stand, I can do no other." A power beyond themselves has absolute claim on them.

There is no rule with regard to the contemplative and the active lives. The gentler spirits may retire from the bustle and violence of the world. Such retirement is not necessarily an escape, for by their contemplative vigour they influence society. We may retire from the world if it is in obedience to an inner urge; it is not right if we do so for fear that we might get entangled in the affairs of the world.

Occasional withdrawal into solitude for short periods every day makes for spiritual growth. There is profound wisdom in the provision for a weekly day of rest and a few minutes of silent meditation every day. But it is not necessary to become monks. As laymen we may have the right attitude. When Anāthapiṇḍika, a wealthy person of his time, proposed to the Buddha to renounce the world, the Buddha said: "I say unto thee, remain in thy station of life and apply thyself with diligence to thy enterprise. It is not life, wealth and power that enslave men but the *cleaving* to life, wealth and power. We are called upon to negate not life and the world but the ego. The relation of man's true self to the transient world is "like the dew-drop on the lotus leaf," [39] touching it but not adhering to it. When one is released from craving and ignorance, one is filled with joy and compassion. A composed mind is the prelude to the compassionate heart which results in right action—*yogaḥ karmasu kauśalam;* yoga is skill in action.

The Yogi and the Commissar are not exclusive of each other. The Yogi acts in the world while remaining a reflective witness of it. He will do his duty in the world without neglecting his higher loyalty. Civilization will justify itself only when men of the world become seers and seers become actors in the world. St. Theresa's words express a great truth: "This is the end of that spiritual union, that there may be born of its working, *works.*"

7. GOD-MEN

By God-men we mean persons like Gautama the Buddha, Jesus the Christ. Their very names express a duality, that they are manifestations of the Spirit through a human medium which is a support of this manifestation. Zarathustra's original name was Spitama while Zarathustra was the title. The Buddha like the Christ indicates the universal reality appear-

---

[39] *Chāndogya Upaniṣad,* IV, 14, 3.

ing in a human manifestation. The question arises in regard
to the relation between the human and the divine aspects of
their nature. The Absolute is reflected in the relative. Each
manifestation is unique, is a relative Absolute, if such a contradiction is permitted. It nevertheless corresponds to a reality.
Man perfected acquires the divine status. He attains the liberation, the freedom which is joy, which is eternity, which is the
truth, the Absolute in which the conflict between the individual and the social ceases.

God-men are the precursors of the truly human. What is
possible for a Gautama or a Jesus is possible for every human
being. The nature of man receives its fulfilment in them. They
are our elder brothers. They show us what humanity is capable
of. The possession of God-consciousness by Gautama or Jesus
does not remove them from other men.[40] Even if we hold that
Jesus is sinless, his humanity is not affected. Sin is not of the
essence of human nature. It is a disturbance or corruption of
it. In us, ordinary human beings, God-consciousness is dark-
ened, enfeebled, imperfectly developed. In Jesus it is absolutely
powerful; the image of God is in full radiance.

The light within is given to every man born into the world.
There is the fragment (aṁśa) or seed (bīja) of the divine
dwelling in the heart, which is capable of regenerating the
whole individual. Each one of us can be delivered from bondage to the world, by whole-hearted trust in the Spirit within.
No blindness or wickedness can destroy the participation in
the Divine.

The saint transformed in God acts as though he were a part

[40] Schleiermacher says: "To ascribe to Christ an absolutely powerful
god-consciousness and to affirm the existence of God in him are exactly
the same thing."

of God. Those who reach perfect union with God will be as much one with God by grace as Jesus when treated as Christ is one with God by nature. The iron turns into fire.

No individual, however great, can be an exhaustive expression of God but each individual is a distinctive expression and brings out a characteristic of God's being. It may be said that every human being is unique and answers to a specific need in God. Existence is an infinite, illimitable reality which figures itself out in a multiplicity of values in life. Each individual is his own authentic self, not a copy of his neighbour, not an instance of a class. Each one has to tread his path. The higher the individuals, the more distinctive are the elements they express. We cannot say that everything in God finds expression in this or that individual, however great he may be.

All human beings come from God and go back to him.[41] We are all the sons of God. Jesus says: "Whoever does the will of my Father in heaven is my brother, and sister, and mother." [42] The point of Jesus' life and teaching is that each one of us can become the son of God. He gives us the clear direction: "You must be perfect, as your heavenly Father is perfect." [43] The Fourth Evangelist says, "But to all who received him, who believed in his name, he gave power to become sons of God, who were born, not of blood nor of the will of the flesh nor of the will of man, but of God." [44] "See what love the Father has given us that we should be called the sons of God" is the joyous cry of John.[45] As long as the cosmic

[41] The Fourth Evangelist makes Jesus say: "I came forth from the Father and am come into the world; again I leave the world and go to the Father."
[42] Matthew 12:50.
[43] Matthew 5:48.
[44] John 1:12–13.

process continues, these souls work for its redemption in close relationship with the Divine.

Both Christianity and Islam start from a theistic standpoint but Christianity insists on the trinitarian aspect. God becomes incarnate and redeems the world. The Divine Principle descends into manifestation to re-establish a disturbed equilibrium. There is a tendency both in the East and in the West to look upon God-men as incarnations of the Supreme. Rāma, the Buddha and Jesus have all been treated as special manifestations of the Supreme.[46] Take, for example, the story of Rāma. Vālmīki, the poet makes him say that he is only a man, the son of Daśaratha,[47] a man who, through suffering, obtained the divine status. But he is traditionally regarded as an incarnation of Viṣṇu. Mālyavān, the maternal grandfather of Rāvaṇa, tells him that he thinks that Rāma is Viṣṇu.[48] In Chapter 72 of the same Kāṇḍa, Rāvaṇa himself looks upon Rāma as the Supreme Godhead.[49] Rāma becomes the symbol of Ultimate Reality in whom the seers delight.[50] An avatāra or incarnation could be of no use to mankind if he were not as other men are, learning as other men do through trial and suffering. If he were God, it would be impossible for us to imitate him. He must be a man like ourselves who has fought and failed and fought again.

The Hindu tradition holds that whenever righteousness de-

[45] I John 3:1.
[46] God said unto Moses: "Thus shalt thou say unto the children of Israel, the Lord God of your fathers, the God of Abraham, of Isaac and of Jacob hath sent me unto you." Exodus 3:15.
[47] ātmānam mānuṣam manye rāmam daśarathātmajam.
[48] viṣṇum manyāmahe rāmam mānuṣaṁ deham āsthitam. *Yuddhakāṇḍa*, 35.
[49] tam manye rāghavam vīram nārāyaṇam anāmayam.
[50] ramante yogino'smin.

clines and unrighteousness increases, there is an outpouring of
divine grace in the birth of a great teacher.[51] The Zoroastrian
Gāthas declare that Zarathustra was born in answer to the
appeal of Mother Earth to the Supreme Ahura-Mazdā. The
Ebionites and perhaps the Nazarenes revered Jesus as the
greatest of the prophets but they did not admit his pre-exist-
ence and divine perfection. To them Jesus appeared to be of
the same species as themselves. His progress from infancy to
youth and then to manhood was marked by a steady increase
in his stature and wisdom. He died on the cross after a painful
agony of body and mind. The prophets of other religions and
ancient days had cured diseases, raised the dead, divided the
sea, stopped the sun and ascended to heaven in a fiery chariot.
Such people were called by the Hebrews the sons of God. Jesus
is a son of God like them.

When the seeds of the faith were spread to Graeco-Roman
soil, whose people were accustomed to a series of angels,
deities, aeons and emanations issuing from the throne of light,
it did not seem incredible to them that the first of these aeons,
the Logos or the Word of God, of the same substance with
God, should descend on earth, and deliver the human race
from vice and error. The Gnostics conceded that the brightest
aeon or emanation of the Deity might assume the outward
shape and visible appearance of a mortal.

But many of the primitive churches could not believe that a
celestial spirit, a portion of the first essence, could get united
with a mass of impure flesh. In their zeal for divinity, they
abjured the humanity of Jesus. The Docetae, for example, denied the truth and authenticity of the Gospels in regard to the
birth of Christ and the first thirty years of his life. It was in-

[51] IV, 7. See also *Bhāgavata*, X, I, 17–18.

conceivable for some of them to believe that their God was in a state of human foetus and emerged at the end of nine months from a woman's womb. For them, he first appeared on the banks of the Jordan in full manhood. The appearance was a form only, not a substance, a figure created by God to imitate the faculties and actions of men. It was all an illusion, a phantom and the scenes of passion and death, resurrection and ascension were acted for the benefit of mankind. When it is urged, comparing Socrates with Jesus, that not a word of impatience and despair escaped the lips of the dying philosopher, it is said in reply that the cry of Jesus "My God, my God, why hast thou forsaken me?" is only apparent.

There were some who believed that Jesus was a mortal like any of us, born of Joseph and Mary. By his own effort he grew to be the best and wisest of the human race. Therefore he was chosen by God to restore on earth true worship of God. When he was baptised in the Jordan, the Christ, the first of the aeons descended on Jesus in the form of a dove, got hold of his mind and directed his activities during the allotted period of his ministry. When Jesus was delivered into the hands of the Jews, the Christ, the immortal aeon, left his earthly tabernacle and flew back to God, leaving Jesus to suffer, complain and die. This was the view of Corinthus and it is grossly unfair to God and man.

The exact nature of the relation between soul and body is difficult to define. It is not more difficult to conceive that an aeon or an archangel may get united with a human body. Apollinaris held that Godhead was united with the body of a human being and the place and function of a human soul were occupied by the Logos.

The Arians argued that the orthodox borrowed their conception of the Trinity from the Valentinians and the Marcionites. They maintained that the Logos was a dependent and spontaneous production, created from nothing by the will of the Father. The Son by whom all things are made has been begotten before all worlds and there had been a time which preceded the ineffable generation of the Logos. God the Father transfused his ample spirit and impressed the effulgence of his glory on this only-begotten son. Being the visible image of the invisible perfection, he governed the world in obedience to the will of the Father. Theophilus, the bishop of Antioch, was the first to employ the word triad or trinity, a term familiar to the schools of philosophy and the Christian doctrine after the middle of the second century.

Praxeus and Sabellius about the end of the second century confounded the Father with the Son and others adhered to the distinction rather than the equality of the two. In the beginning of the fifth century the unity of the two natures was accepted as a mystery which we cannot explain by our ideas or express in our language. To question it is blasphemy.[52] Prior to the Council of Nicaea no creed had ever been formulated which was to be regarded as a test of orthodoxy.

Even as the historical Jesus was elevated in Christian teaching into the "glorified Christ," so Gautama the Buddha became more than the human being and was worshipped as the Lord and Saviour. As the Christian doctrine developed into the Trinity, Buddhism adopted the Trikāya or the threefold body. Dharmakāya is the unconditioned spiritual reality, the essence of enlightenment and compassion. It is the Absolute

---

[52] "May those who divide Christ be divided with the sword, may they be hewn in pieces, may they be burned alive" was the verdict of a Christian synod.

Reality which every individual has to realise for himself. Sambhoga Kāya is the body of bliss, the personification of wisdom, the Absolute individualised in the true eternal Buddha. Nirmāṇakāya is the body of transformation, the embodied Buddha, the historical Gautama the Buddha, who partakes of all the characteristics of mortal flesh. The Buddha is not three but one. The three are aspects of the one Reality.

Mahāyāna Buddhism like the *Bhagavadgītā* makes out that the Buddhas appear on earth for the redemption of mankind. "The exalted one appears in the world for salvation to many people, for joy to many people, out of compassion for the world, as a blessing, as a salvation, as the joy of gods and men."[53]

Christians contend that the revelation of God in Jesus Christ is essentially different in kind from all other divine expressions, in nature, history, individual human souls, that it is the one and only act of revelation, the one and only occasion in which God has come in person to this earth. Between the unique event of incarnation in Jesus and the other operations of God, there is no "historical continuity of revelation" according to Brunner.[54] This is an entirely unique event in which God has acted and spoken once for all and only once on the stage of human history.

No incarnation need be regarded as an isolated act of divine intervention. Karl Barth's conviction that there is no direct continuity between God and man misrepresents the teaching of Jesus that God is the Father of us all and there is a common element between us. The Logos doctrine is the basis of Christianity. It implies that God has revealed himself at sundry

---

[53] *Sad-dharma puṇḍarīka*, XV.
[54] *The Mediator*, Eng. translation (1924), p. 25.

times and in diverse manners. The Christian revelation is not something different from all others. The epigram of St. Athanasius that "God became man in order that we might become divine" suggests the community of spirit between God and man. The Incarnation is an act which goes on continually. Athanasius remarks: "All those in whom the Holy Ghost abides become deified by this reason alone." [55] God generously participates in the history of the world. The *Bhagavadgītā* puts the case of the continuous activity of the Divine. "Whenever there is a decline of righteousness and rise of unrighteousness, then I send forth [incarnate] myself." [56] This activity of the Divine will go on until the whole world becomes one divine incarnation. At the heart of reality there is overflowing love.

There is a sense in which each incarnation is unique. It is unique in relation to its context. Each of the manifestations reflects the nature of God.[57]

Islam does not give the same predominance to the mediator as Christianity does. To a Muslim, all is centred in Allāh. The

[55] *Ep. ad Scrap,* 1.24.

[56] IV.7.

[57] Hastings Rashdall writes: "It is impossible to maintain that God is fully incarnate in Jesus Christ and not incarnate at all in anyone else." *God and Man* (1910), p. 75. Archbishop William Temple wrote: "By the word of God—that is to say by Jesus Christ—Isaiah and Plato, Zoroaster, Buddha and Confucius uttered and wrote such truths as they declared. There is only one Divine Light, and every man in his own measure is enlightened by it." *Readings in St. John's Gospel* (1939), Vol. I, p. 10. Christianity has never affirmed that "Jesus of Nazareth, in the days of his flesh, is God's final word in human history." Bishop F. R. Barry: *The Relevance of the Christs* (1935), p. 70. "It is absurd," says Archbishop Soderblom of Upsala, "to look upon revelation as finished with Christ." *The Living God* (1931), p. 351. For J. M. Creed Christianity contains not all the truth but the deepest truth. See *The Divinity of Christ* (1938), p. 112.

idea of God made man is at the centre of Christianity. The Son, the second person of the Trinity, is man universalised. Jesus Christ is God individualised. In Islam every man is his own priest by the mere fact of his being a Muslim. He is the image of the Creator whose vicar (*Khalīfah*) he is on earth. The inward and divine reality of God-men is the same. Eckhart observes: "Everything that the Holy scriptures say about Christ is equally true of every good and divine man."

8

Interreligious Friendship

1. THE TRANSCENDENT UNITY OF RELIGIONS

THE seers, whatever be their religion, ask us to rise to the conception of a God above gods, who is beyond image and concept, who can be experienced but not known, who is the vitality of the human spirit and the ultimacy of all that exists. This goal represents the transcendent unity of religions which is above their empirical diversity.

The differences among religions seem prominent because we do not seem to know the basic truth of our own religions. There is a common element in all religious experience, a common foundation on which it rests its faith and worship. But the building that is erected on this foundation differs with each individual. God's architecture is not of a standard pattern. The lives of religious people bear ample testimony to it. The gifts of God's spirit to men are as varied as men are varied. St. Paul speaks of the Spirit as dividing his gifts "to every man severally as he will." The experience of each individual is, in some sense, unique. Each has to discover God for himself; each has to bring his own special contribution to the common fund. The variety of experience adds to the spiritual richness of the world.

The unity of the different religions cannot be achieved at

the external level. It has to be realised in an inward and spiritual way without prejudice to any particular forms. The Hindu seer has no contempt for other religions. He looks upon them as aids to our knowledge of God, as channels of divine revelation. He does not believe that salvation is to be had only through any one particular religion. God does not refuse his truth, his love and his grace to any who, in sincerity, seek him, wherever they may be and whatever creeds they may profess.

In *The Spirit of Prayer,* William Law makes out that differences of religion are on the surface. "There is but one possible way for man to attain this salvation, of life of God in the soul. There is not one for the Jew, another for a Christian and a third for the heathen. No: God is one, human nature is one, salvation is one, and the way to it is one; that is the desire of the soul turned to God. . . . Thus does this desire do all, it brings the soul to God, and is one life with God. Suppose this desire not to be alive, not in motion either in a Jew or a Christian, then all the sacrifices, the service, the worship either of the Law or the Gospel, are but dead works, that bring no life into the soul, nor beget any union between God and it. Suppose this desire to be awakened, and fixed upon God, though in souls that never heard either of the Law or the Gospel, then the Divine life, or operation of God enters into them and the new birth in Christ is formed in those who never heard of His Name." [1]

Those who are anchored in the truth are convinced of the relativity of doctrines about God or ways to reach him. Hindu scriptures affirm that we use words to get beyond words, to reach the pure wordless essence. The Hindu tradition refuses to reduce religious experience to a dead level of uniformity.

[1] *Works of William Law,* Vol. VII, p. 46.

Truth, for Hinduism, is a reality experienced, a light which breaks through the transcendent in man into the partial world reflected by sense and intellect, the world of objectification in which the light is dimmed. The contradictions of theological thought arise when we apply to the spiritual life conceptions drawn from and suitable only to the life of this world. To identify the truth with the intellectual form is the sin of rationalism, which is insensitive to the meaning of creative mystery and to the primary spiritual experience in the existential subject in which truth and revelation are one. Those who have had this experience are remote from atheism as much as from unimaginative theism which is lost in outworn and distorted forms of the knowledge of God.

Raising the question whether God-realisation, *brahmaprāpti,* is limited to the Vedic seers, Vātsyāyana, commenting on the *Nyāya Sūtra,* says that it is found among the Aryans and the non-Aryans, *ṛṣi-arya-mlecchānām samānam lakṣaṇam.* They were not inclined to be shut up in their own language, culture and tradition. Historic events that shape other parts of the world should also move us. "All that is true, by whomsoever it has been said, is from the Holy Ghost," said St. Ambrose.[2] The institutions of religions should be so organised as to give their adherents spiritual opportunities to live the kind of life expected of them.

Kabir, the fifteenth-century apostle of Hindu-Muslim unity, said: "The Hindu God lives at Benares; the Muslim God at Mecca. But He who made the world lives not in a city made by hands. There is one Father of Hindu and Muslim, one God in all matter."

The Buddha was opposed to all those who had set views or

[2] Comment on I Corinthians 12:3. This view is endorsed by Thomas Aquinas. *Summa Theologica,* I, II, 109, 110.

closed systems of thought. He insisted that his followers should concentrate on the way leading to enlightenment. If we adopt definite views, we get concerned about defending them. This leads to disputations with rival doctrines, resulting in pride. The true seer has shaken off all views. Having no view to defend, no prejudice to plead, he is free from doctrinairism. In Mahāyāna Buddhism, the goal of enlightenment may be reached by many means, *upāya*. Any way which relieves us of our spiritual blindness and leads to enlightenment is permissible. When the teacher uses ideas and words in his instruction, he uses them "in the resemblance of a raft that is of use only to cross a river." It is said that to be born in a church is good but one should not die in it. The easy course for man is to follow established usage, conform to general forms of human existence. He becomes one among many leading an easy life, clinging to old forms or outmoded ideas at the expense of his personal dignity and authenticity.

Micah says: "Let every man walk in the name of his God, and we will walk in the name of our God." Respect for other views of God is a mark of authentic religious life.

There is the liberal view in Christianity also. Clement argues that the Greeks were led to Christ through philosophy and the Hebrews through law.[3] Even so other schools of religion contain fragments of truth which may be supplemented by Christianity. He maintains that Plato and his followers were able to attain to a knowledge of God as Father though not of the Son or the Spirit.[4]

Justin Martyr and the Christian philosophers of Alexandria of the second and third centuries held that Christ, the Eternal Word of God, had been truly speaking in the hearts of great

[3] See *De Principe,* I, II, 2, 11, 7.
[4] *Stromata,* I, 5, 13.

O

souls long before the birth of Jesus, in Socrates and Plato as well as in Abraham and Jesus. "Christ is the reason of whom every race of men partakes: and those who live according to reason are really Christians, even though they may be called atheists. Such were Socrates and Heraclitus among the Greeks and others like them; and among the barbarians [i.e., non-Greeks] Abraham, Elijah . . . etc." [5] Again: "Stoics, poets, prose-writers, each spoke well through his share in a little seed of the Divine Reason. So, whatever has been spoken well by any men, really belongs to us Christians." [6]

Islam is called "Deen-ul-Ḥaqq," the religion of truth. It does not claim that it has the sole monopoly of truth. The Quran says: "We believe in God and the revelation given to us and to Abraham and Ishmail, Isaac, Jacob and that given to Moses and Jesus and that given to other apostles from their Lord. We make no difference between them." [7] The Quran affirms that "There is no people among whom a warner has not been sent." Islam asks its followers to recognise the prophets of other religions. It is unfair to God's love and mercy to assume that he left millions of men to stagnate for thousands of years, practically without hope in the darkness of ignorance.

The lives lived and not the words spoken reveal whether our faith is authentic or spurious. By their fruits ye shall know them. [8] A controversy arose in the Primitive Christian Church

[5] I. *Apology,* XLVI.
[6] II *Apology,* XIII.
[7] II, 136.
[8] Matthew 7:16.
William Blake:
> "And all must love the human form,
> In heathen, Turk or Jew;
> Where Mercy, Love and Pity dwell
> There God is dwelling too."

over the question of circumcision and it was decided not by an appeal to texts but by a reference to experience. "If their God gave the same gift to them [the uncircumcised heathens] as he gave to us [the circumcised Jews] . . . who was I that I could withstand God?" [9] William Penn, the Quaker founder of Pennsylvania, wrote: "The humble, meek, merciful, just, pious and devout souls are everywhere of one religion; and when death has taken off the mask, they will know one another, though the diverse liveries they wear here make them strangers." Nicholas Berdyaev said: "Christians may very well recognise that the Hindu, the Buddhist, the Jew, the Muslim, the free-thinking spiritualist, if they strive after God, the spiritual life, truth and goodness, may be much nearer to God and Christ than the outward adepts of Christianity." [10]

[9] The Directors of the East India Company opposed Christian missionary activities on the ground, among others, that it would interfere with the Hindu religion, which produced "men of the purest morality and strictest virtue." See J. C. Marshman, *Life and Times of Carey, Marshman and Ward* (1859), p. 46.

When a suggestion was made that the people were "sunk in the grossest brutality" and should be reformed religiously, Warren Hastings wrote that the Hindus "are as exempt from the worst propensities of human nature as any people on the face of the eart', ourselves not excepted. They are gentle, benevolent, more susceptible of gratitude for kindness shown them than prompt to vengeance for wrongs sustained, abhorrent of bloodshed, faithful and affectionate in service and submission to legal authority. They are superstitious; but they do not think ill of us for not behaving as they do. Coarse as the modes of their worship are, the precepts of their religion are admirably fitted to promote the peace and good order of society; and even from their theology arguments, which no other can afford, may be drawn to support the most refined mysteries of our own. . . . The least that can be expected from the most liberal and enlightened of all nations is to protect their persons from wrong, and to leave their religious creed to the Being who has so long endured it, and who will, in his own time, reform it."

[10] *Faiths and Fellowship* (1936), p. 79. Cf. Jacques Maritain: "The saying 'No salvation outside the Church' can shock only those who are ignorant of the soul of the Church. All it means to us is that there is no salvation outside the Truth." *Redeeming the Time* (1943), pp. 105 ff.

The variety of creeds does not repudiate the truth of religion. The formulations are relative to the context of the historical and geographical knowledge of the age in which they are formulated. Without the assistance of these formulations, religions cannot develop. W. R. Inge's words are not without significance. "Pieces of obsolete science, imprisoned like a fly in amber, in the solid mass of religious creed, may have become the casket in which the soul keeps her most valued treasures." Myths and legends serve as symbols.

The notions of God framed by men are not God himself. Mental images are necessary to bring Godhead into human understanding but they are only images and symbols, historical, inadequate. Kant argues that religious dogmas are only ideas to regulate our reason, heuristic fictions, symbols of an inscrutable reality of which we are unable to know what it is in itself though we can know what it means to us.

If anyone feels that he was led to the perception of Divine Reality through the Buddha, Jesus or Muhammad, he cannot help telling others about it. Jesus asks his disciples after the Resurrection: "Go and make disciples of all nations." [11] "Go into all the world and preach the Gospel to every creature." [12] Whether these words were uttered by Jesus or not, the early Church believed them. Take the words of St. Peter: "There is no other name given under heaven whereby we must be saved, but only in the name of our Lord Jesus Christ." This cannot be taken literally in view of the undoubted experience of the presence of the Spirit of God among men who are Hindu, Buddhist, Jew or Muslim. All outer names are man-made distinctions whereas the reality is faith in God and love

[11] Matthew 28:19.
[12] Mark 16:15.

of man. It is not necessary to do away with the differences which distinguish and divide men. We should try to understand them. We must admit faith in the one God of all mankind who is worshipped in many ways.

A truly religious man has a sense of humility. He has faith but not fanaticism. He submits to the reality felt by him and is aware that his particular view may be inadequate. The fanatic has no sense of inadequacy. While faith is the refuge of the humble, fanaticism is the outcome of a secret and excessive pride. While one can say that the revelation one had is completely satisfying, one cannot say that there has been no other revelation in the past and that there will be no other in the future. It is not faith but fanaticism that asserts that one's own revelation contains all the truth about God that has ever been made known to man in the past and that no further truth ever will or can be made known in the future.[13]

2. CHRISTIAN REUNION

In each of the living faiths, sects have grown up which have

[13] Cf. Charles E. Raven: "It is precisely this claim to an absolute finality whether in the Church or the Scriptures or in Jesus Christ or in anything else, this claim that revelation belongs to a totally different order of reality from discovery or that a creed is something more than a working hypothesis, that perplexes and affronts those of us who have a proper sense of our own limitations. We can be utterly convinced as we encounter Christ that He expresses for us in terms of human life the quality of God, that He fulfils and surpasses all that we know or can conceive of God, that abstractions like the Absolute, or the Life force, or the Soul of the World are idolatrous beside Him, that we can and must offer to Him adoration and penitence, that He is for us 'of one substance with the Father.' But we cannot, if we are to be truthful, say more than that He is God for us; for this is the most that in our finite and human state we can say of any such conviction; God for us, God in the sense in which alone we can understand and use the term, God in so far as His being and nature can be reflected in the perfect Son of Man." *Natural Religion and Christian Theology* (1953).

developed the illusion of being infallibly right in their interpretations of the faith and there are attempts at a reunion of the
sects.

In the middle of January, 1946, was published the report
of the commission appointed by the Archbishop of Canterbury
"to survey the whole problem of modern evangelism with special reference to the spiritual needs and prevailing intellectual
outlook of the non-worshipping members of the community
and to report on the organisation and methods by which the
needs can most effectively be met." This report entitled "The
Conversion of England" points out that religion has become
a waning influence in the national life of the country "which
is still Christian on the surface." There is a decline in moral
standards, "in truthfulness and personal honesty and an
alarming spread of sexual laxity and of the gambling fever."
Decline in church attendance is but one symptom of the
change in the outlook of modern men, which is increasingly
sceptical and secular. While the times call for a strengthening
and quickening of spiritual life, the present leadership has
become confused and uncertain. The report deplores the unhappy divisions, the lack of charity among particular congre-
gations, which obscure the fellowship of the Christian Church
and calls upon t e different Christian sects to combine and
co-operate in the task of the conversion of England.[14] The
movements which make for Christian unity adopt the principle of unity with variety, which is not only a profound
spiritual truth but the most obvious common sense. But the

[14] *The World Conference on Faith and Order* which met in Edinburgh in August, 1937, declared in the "Affirmation of Unity": "We
humbly acknowledge that our divisions are contrary to the will of Christ,
and we pray God in His mercy to shorten the days of our separation and
to guide us by His spirit into fulness of unity."

attempt should not stop at the frontiers of Christianity. It should take a larger view. Secularism and paganism present a growing menace not only to the Christian way of life but to the religious outlook as such. They offer the rivalries of religions as a proof of the futility of religion.

The principle that is inspiring the movement for the reunion of Christian churches should be extended to the union of the great living faiths of mankind. In the sphere of religion also, there is room for diversity and no need for discord. If the sects of Christianity can get together, giving up their claims for the exclusive possession of the truth of Christianity, it is not too much to hope that Christianity itself may modify its claim for the exclusive possession of spiritual truth. Belief in such exclusive claims and monopolies of religious truth has been a frequent source of religious pride and fanaticism and a formidable obstacle to co-operation in the world of spirit.

If we reflect on the matter deeply, we will perceive the unity of spiritual aspiration and endeavour underlying the varied upward paths indicated in the different world faiths. The diversity in the historical formulations of the fundamental spiritual truths tends to diminish as we climb up the scale of spiritual perfection. All the paths of ascent lead to the hilltop. This convergent tendency and the remarkable degree of agreement in the witness of those who reach the hilltop are the strongest proof of the truth of religion. Emphasis on this fundamental spiritual outlook, which characterises the living religions of the world, is essential for the world order and peace which cannot be realised by political and economic planning alone. To neglect the spiritual unity of the world and underline the religious diversity would be philosophically unjustifiable, morally indefensible and socially dangerous. Where there is the spirit of the Lord, there is unity.

If we are to remove the present disordered, divided, state of the religious world, we have to adopt what William Law calls "a catholic spirit, a communion of saints in the love of God and all goodness, which no one can learn from that which is called orthodoxy in particular churches, but is only to be had by a total dying to all worldly views, by a pure love of God, and by such an unction from above as delivers the mind from all selfishness and makes it love truth and goodness with an equality of affection in every man, whether he is Christian, Jew or Gentile."

The great Buddhist emperor Aśoka, in his twelfth edict, proclaimed: "His Sacred Majesty the King does reverence to men of all sects, whether ascetics or householders, by gifts and various forms of reverence. His Sacred Majesty however cares not so much for gifts or external reverence as that there should be a growth in the essence of the matter in all sects. . . . He who does reverence to his own sect, while disparaging the sects of others, wholly from attachment to his own, with intent to enhance the glory of his own sect, in reality, by such conduct, inflicts the severest injury on his own sect. Concord therefore is meritorious, to wit, hearkening and hearkening willingly to the Law of Piety, as accepted by other people." Only in such a way will it be possible for us to develop a common or corporate spiritual life for the world as a whole. Only then will religion be able to attract those humanists, those loyal servants of their fellow men who are unable today to profess any faith, without sacrifice of their intellectual and ethical conscience.

Interests of truth are dependent on freedom of thought. It is through an appreciation of other ideas that we attain an increased apprehension of truth. Even if other ideas are erroneous it is good for truth to struggle with error. Nothing is more fatal to truth than suppression of error by force. If we suppress freedom of thought, deal with conscientious expression of one's ideas by Inquisition or Index, by arbitrary governmental action, by unjust economic or social pressures, we depart from religious truth and democratic ideals. "Compel them to come in" has no meaning in religion or politics. Religion is an attitude which gives meaning and unity to existence and is not a set of dogmas to be universally accepted. Dogmas and rites, even religions, are not ends in themselves. They are instruments to carry forward God's purpose for mankind. They should not become servants of any one class or culture, race or nation. It is unwise to ask people to abandon the traditions which have lasted for thousands of years, which have provided spiritual support of innumerable generations and have produced saints of wisdom and holiness. Ideas have a life of their own even as a plant has a life of its own so long as it is rooted in the soil.

Religions today may learn more from each other than they did in the past, though no one of them however modified by contact with others is likely to provide a basis acceptable to all for the spiritual unification of mankind. But the higher religions tend to converge if we look to the spiritual facts on which they are based and the moral universalism which they teach. We can draw inspiration from more than one of the existing religions. We do not want a new religion but we need a new and enlarged understanding of the old religions. The future of religion is bound up not with the acceptance of one religion by all or a state of conflict or anarchy among religions or vague incongruous eclecticism but the acceptance of a fundamental unity with a free differentiation.

Our unity is of the heart and spirit. We are divided in the outward forms of our life in God, but we believe that a deeper understanding of the different forms will lead to a united comprehension of the truth of spiritual life. This view is stressed by people who dwell far apart in time or space and this distance need not prove an obstacle to our participation in their bounty, for it has the power to help us to win back our own lost inheritance.[15]

The indifference, if not contempt, which many of us have for religions other than our own, is due to ignorance and incomprehension. If we study them with reverence, we will realise that they share a sympathy of outlook. By living not merely in splendid isolation but in active hostility, they have lost a great opportunity. "It is a reproach to us that with our unique opportunities of entering into sympathetic relations with Indian thought, we have made few attempts to do so. . . . I am not suggesting that we should become Buddhists or Hindus, but I believe that we have almost as much to learn from them as they from us." [16] If God be the God of all mankind, even

---

[15] A mediaeval Indian mystic wrote: "There may be different kinds of oil in different lamps, the wicks may also be of different kinds, but when they burn, we have the same flame and illumination."

[16] *Mysticism in Religion,* W. R. Inge (1947), p. 8.

R. G. Collingwood writes: "Above these jarrings and creakings of the machines of thought, there is a melody sung in unison by the spirits of the spheres, which are the great philosophers. This melody is not a body of truth revealed once for all, but a living thought whose content, never discovered for the first time, is progressively determined and clarified by every genuine thinker." *Speculum Mentis* (1924), p. 13.

Whitehead in his *Religion in the Making* (1926) writes: "The decay of Christianity and Buddhism, as determinative influences in modern thought, is partly due to the fact that each religion has unduly sheltered itself from the other. The self-sufficient pedantry of learning and the confidence of ignorant zealots have combined to shut up each religion in its own forms of thought. Instead of looking to each other for deeper meanings, they have remained self-satisfied and unfertilised." P. 146.

those who belong to other groups and use other idioms are grappling with the same ultimate questions. Mr. C. F. Andrews said: "If Christianity is to succeed, it must not come forward as an antagonist and a rival to the great religious strivings of the past. It must come as a helper and a fulfiller, a peacemaker and a friend. There must no longer be the desire to capture converts from Hinduism, but to come to her aid in the needful time of trouble, and to help her in the fulfilment of duties she has long neglected." [17]

Religions by working on each other should help them all to attain a great vision of human fellowship. Dr. Albert Schweitzer says: "Western and Indian philosophies must not contend in the spirit that aims at the one proving itself right in opposition to the other. Both must be moving towards a way of thinking which shall . . . eventually be shared in common by all mankind." [18] They are friends and partners in the pursuit of spiritual life. All religions are bound together in a holy partnership to advance the cause of peace, justice and freedom. The love of our brethren must pass into the love of our neighbours.[19] The religion of spirit must keep alive the stir of spiritual fellowship.

Each of the great religions, though not originally at least by importation from other religions, has more or less the same religious ideas.

"In a world materially linked together by the many inventions of Western technique, Hinduism and the Mahāyāna might make no less fruitful contributions than Isis-worship and neo-Platonism had once made to Christian insight and practice." Arnold J. Toynbee: *A Study of History* (1954), Vol. VII, p. 107.

[17] *India in Transition* (1910).

[18] George Seaver: *Albert Schweitzer* (1947), p. 276.

[19] "God loveth the stranger in giving him food and raiment; love ye therefore the stranger, for ye were strangers in the land of Egypt." *Deuteronomy* 10:18, 19.

When India is said to be a secular state, it does not mean that we reject the reality of an Unseen Spirit or the relevance of religion to life or that we exalt irreligion. It does not mean that secularism itself becomes a positive religion or that the State assumes divine prerogatives. Though faith in the Supreme is the basic principle of the Indian tradition, the Indian state will not identify itself with or be controlled by any particular religion. We hold that no one religion should be given preferential status, or unique distinction, that no one religion should be accorded special privileges in national life or international relations for that would be a violation of the basic principles of democracy and contrary to the best interests of religion and government. This view of religious impartiality, of comprehension and forbearance, has a prophetic role to play within the national and the international life. No group of citizens shall arrogate to itself rights and privileges which it denies to others. No person should suffer any form of disability or discrimination because of his religion but all alike should be free to share to the fullest degree in the common life. This is the basic principle involved in the separation of Church and State. The religious impartiality of the Indian state is not to be confused with secularism or atheism. Secularism as here defined is in accordance with the ancient religious tradition of India. It tries to build up a fellowship of believers, not by subordinating individual qualities to the group mind but by bringing them into harmony with each other. This dynamic fellowship is based on the principle of diversity in unity which alone has the quality of creativeness.

A study of different religions indicates that they have philosophical depth, spiritual intensity, vigour of thought, human sympathy. Holiness, purity, chastity and charity are not the exclusive possessions of any religion in the world.

In every religion today we have small minorities who see beyond the horizons of their particular faith, who believe that religious fellowship is possible, not through the imposition of any one way on the whole world but through an all-inclusive recognition that we are all searchers for the truth, pilgrims on the road, that we all aim at the same ethical and spiritual standards. Those who thirst for a first-hand experience are the prophets of the religion of spirit, which is independent of all ecclesiastical organisations, and the subtleties engendered by human learning, which looks for the formation of an earthly community governed by love. The widespread existence of this state of mind is the hope of the future.[20]

[20] Mr. Lawrence Hyde observes: "Amidst all the conflict and confusions, the sympathetic observer can trace the emerging outlines of a new form of religion . . . what may prove to be the ground-plan of the Temple in which our spiritual descendants are destined to worship. The structure which thus discloses itself is *absolutely fundamental*—that of Wisdom Religion which by a *metaphysical necessity* must provide the interior key to all exterior symbolisations and observances. . . . The great majority of those who are finding their way back to religion, from scepticism and materialism, are not returning to the faith of their fathers, but to some form of the Wisdom Religion." *The Wisdom Religion Today*. (Burning-Glass Paper No. 13, pp. 44 ff., quoted in E. C. Dewick. *The Christian Attitude to Other Religions* (1953), p. 19.)

Conclusion

THOUGH our age has largely ceased to understand the meaning of religion, it is still in desperate need of that which religion alone can give. The recognition of a Transcendent Supreme, the freedom of the human individual as a manifestation of the Supreme and the unity of mankind as the goal of history are the foundations of the major religions. The religion of spirit reasserts these fundamental truths. It does not regard dogmas and rites as anything more than a necessarily inadequate symbolism. It calls upon the leaders of religions to set in motion a process of fermentation that will preserve the faiths from hardening into moulds of orthodoxy, religious and social. The religion outlined in these pages may be called the *sanātana dharma,* the eternal religion. It is not to be identified with any particular religion, for it is the religion which transcends race and creed and yet informs all races and creeds. We can so transform the religion to which we belong as to make it approximate to the religion of spirit. I am persuaded that every religion has possibilities of such a transformation.[1]

[1] Professor Louis Renou writes: "The troubles of the present age, which are rightly or wrongly attributed to Western materialism, have helped to increase the prestige of Hinduism. Some people see it as the authentic survival of a tradition, or rather, of the one Tradition, and make it the basis of their *philosophia perennis.* Others try to incorporate it in a universal religious syncretism. Whether these attempts will succeed must be left for the future to decide. The fact remains that Hinduism provides an incomparable field of study for the historian of religion: its aberrations are many, but there is in it a great stream of mystical power; it manifests all the conceptions of religion, and its speculation is con-

We must look upon Hinduism or Christianity as part of an evolving revelation that might in time be taken over into the larger religion of the spirit.

We live in an age of tension, danger and opportunity. We are aware of our insufficiencies, and can remove them if we have the vision to see the goal and the courage to work for it.

---

tinually revealing them in a new light. It combines powers of constant renewal with a firm conservancy of fundamental tradition. In Bhakti and still more in Yoga, it has perfected unrivalled techniques of mystical initiation, that contrast strongly with the frequently haphazard methods of spiritual training in the West. Above all, in the interpenetration of religion and dharma in general and the reciprocal stimulus of abstract thought and religious experiment, there is an underlying principle that, given favourable conditions, may well lead to a new integration of the human personality." *Religions of Ancient India* (1953), p. 110.